I0617560

To my mother who taught me the love for music ☺

A mi madre quien me inculcó el amor por la música ☺

BOOK 2: MUSIC NOTES

Kodaly Signs

Music Notes are sounds with different pitches. Music Notes can be high or low. They may also go up, go down or repeat themselves. We will use the Kodaly method that makes use of different hand gestures to indicate the height of each music note and thus begin to train our musical ear.

Music Staff and Treble Clef

We will learn to draw the five horizontal lines called the **Staff** and the **Treble Clef.**

On the staff we will learn to draw the notes on the **lines** and within the **spaces** in Treble Clef.

Musical Family in Treble Clef and Intervals

With the names of the Musical Family, we will learn to memorize the notes and, in this way, we will learn to **read the music**!

This Musical Family is made up of: **Do**ny, the father, **Re**xi, the mother, **Mi**mi, the grandma, **Fa**fi, the grandpa, **Sol**ti, the little brother, **La**la, the aunt, **Si**si, the little sister and **Do**di, the baby brother.

We will only use the first syllable of each name and in this fun way we will learn the name of the notes: **Do, Re, Mi, Fa, Sol, La, Si, Do.**

The **interval i**s the distance between two notes. They are like "jumps". To know the name of the interval we will count how many notes there are in that jump.

TO REMEMBER

- ➤ Kodaly Signs
- ➤ Music Staff
- ➤ Treble Clef
- ➤ Music Notes
- ➤ Intervals

LIBRO 2: NOTAS MUSICALES

Signos Kodaly   p. 4

Las **Notas Musicales** son sonidos con alturas diferentes. Las notas pueden ser altas o bajas. También suben, bajan o se repiten. Utilizaremos el método Kodaly que hace uso de diferentes gestos de las manos para indicar la altura de cada nota musical y así empezar a entrenar nuestro oído musical.

El Pentagrama y la Clave de Sol   p. 8

Aprenderemos a trazar las cinco líneas horizontales llamadas **Pentagrama** y la **Clave de Sol**. En el Pentagrama aprenderemos a dibujar las notas sobre las **líneas** y dentro de los **espacios** en la Clave de Sol.

La Familia Musical en Clave de Sol y los Intervalos   p. 13

Con los nombres de la Familia Musical aprenderemos a memorizar las notas y de esta manera a **leer la música!**

Esta Familia Musical se compone de: **Do**ny, el papá, **Re**xi, la mamá, **Mi**mi, la abuelita, **Fa**fi, el abuelito, **Sol**ti, el hermanito, **La**la, la tía, **Si**si, la hermanita y **Do**di, el hermanito bebé.

Solo utilizaremos la primera sílaba de cada nombre y de esta manera divertida aprenderemos el nombre de las notas: **Do, Re, Mi, Fa, Sol, La, Si, Do.**

El **intervalo** es la distancia que hay entre dos notas. Son como "saltos". Para conocer el nombre del intervalo contaremos cuántas notas hay en ese salto.

PARA RECORDAR

➤ Signos Kodaly

➤ Pentagrama

➤ Clave de Sol

➤ Notas Musicales

➤ Intervalos

The notes go up, go down or repeat themselves
(Like the balloons)

Las notas suben, bajan o se repiten
(Como las pelotas)

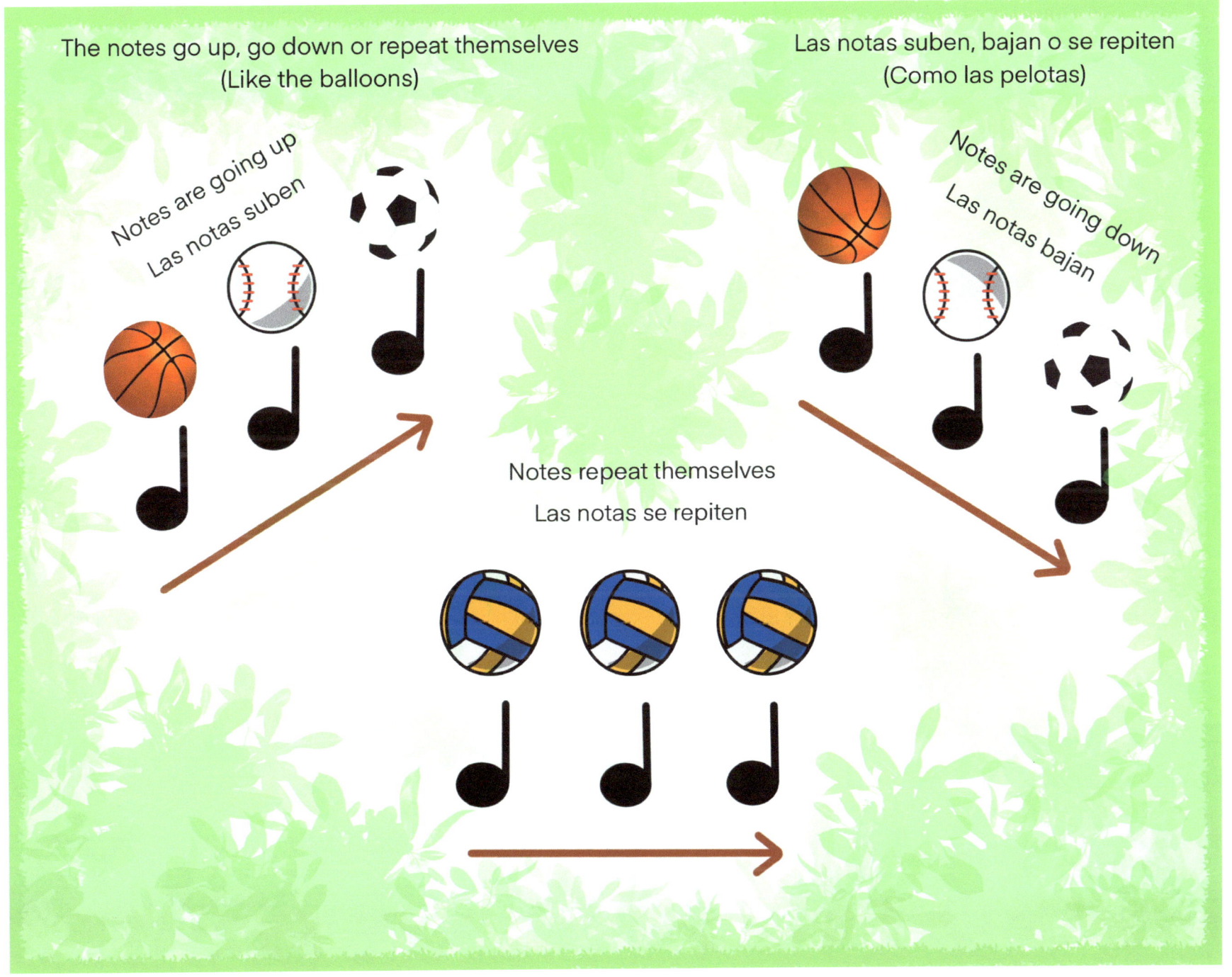

Notes are going up
Las notas suben

Notes are going down
Las notas bajan

Notes repeat themselves

Las notas se repiten

Let's practice the notes that go up, go down or repeat themselves

Practiquemos las notas que suben, que bajan o que se repiten

Let's practice with the planets the notes and KODALY signs going up

Practiquemos con los planetas las notas y los signos KODALY que van subiendo

Count 5 lines and 4 spaces on the **STAFF** by sliding your finger from right to left or left to right

Cuente 5 líneas y 4 espacios en el **PENTAGRAMA** deslizando el dedo de derecha a izquierda o de izquierda a derecha

TREBLE CLEF ON THE 5 LINES

Slide your finger on the treble clef

CLAVE DE SOL SOBRE LAS 5 LÍNEAS

Deslice su dedo sobre la clave de Sol

How to draw the treble clef

Cómo dibujar la clave de sol

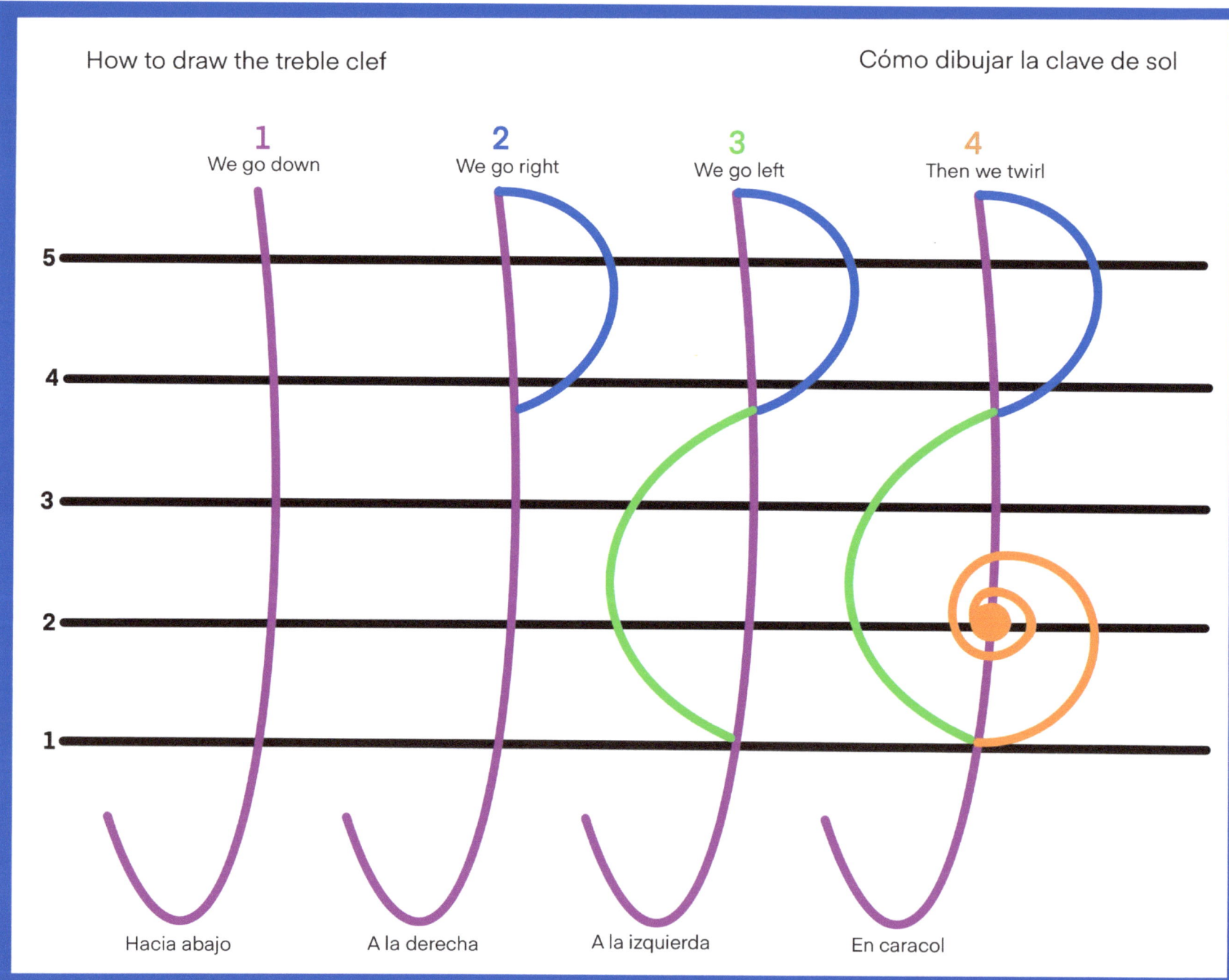

1 We go down — Hacia abajo

2 We go right — A la derecha

3 We go left — A la izquierda

4 Then we twirl — En caracol

STAFF

The house of the notes

PENTAGRAMA

La casa de las notas

Count 5 lines and 4 spaces Cuente 5 líneas y 4 espacios

Music notes can be placed on, above, below or between the lines

Las notas musicales pueden colocarse sobre, encima, debajo o entre las líneas

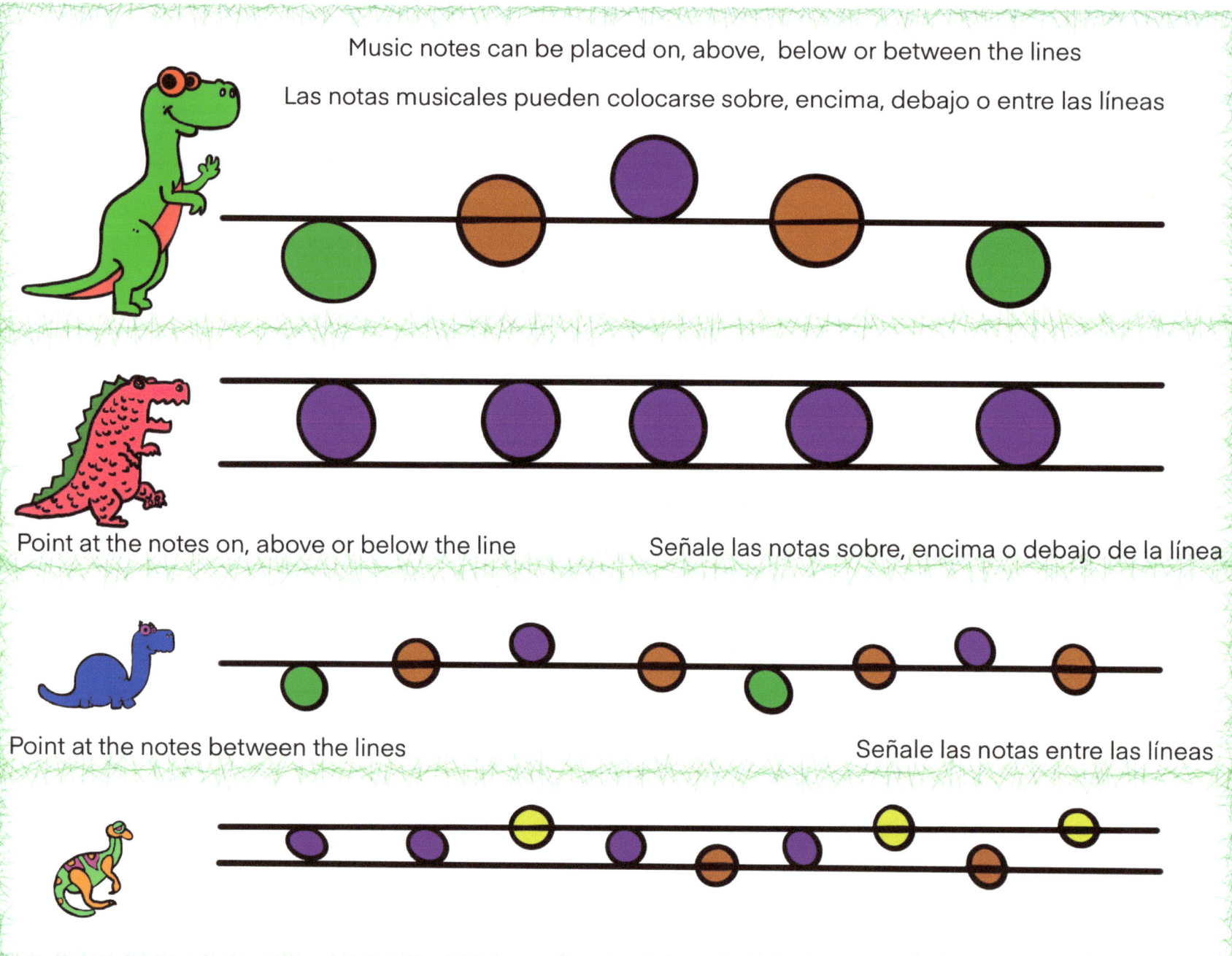

Point at the notes on, above or below the line

Señale las notas sobre, encima o debajo de la línea

Point at the notes between the lines

Señale las notas entre las líneas

THE FAMILY OF THE MUSIC NOTES

LA FAMILIA DE LAS NOTAS MUSICALES

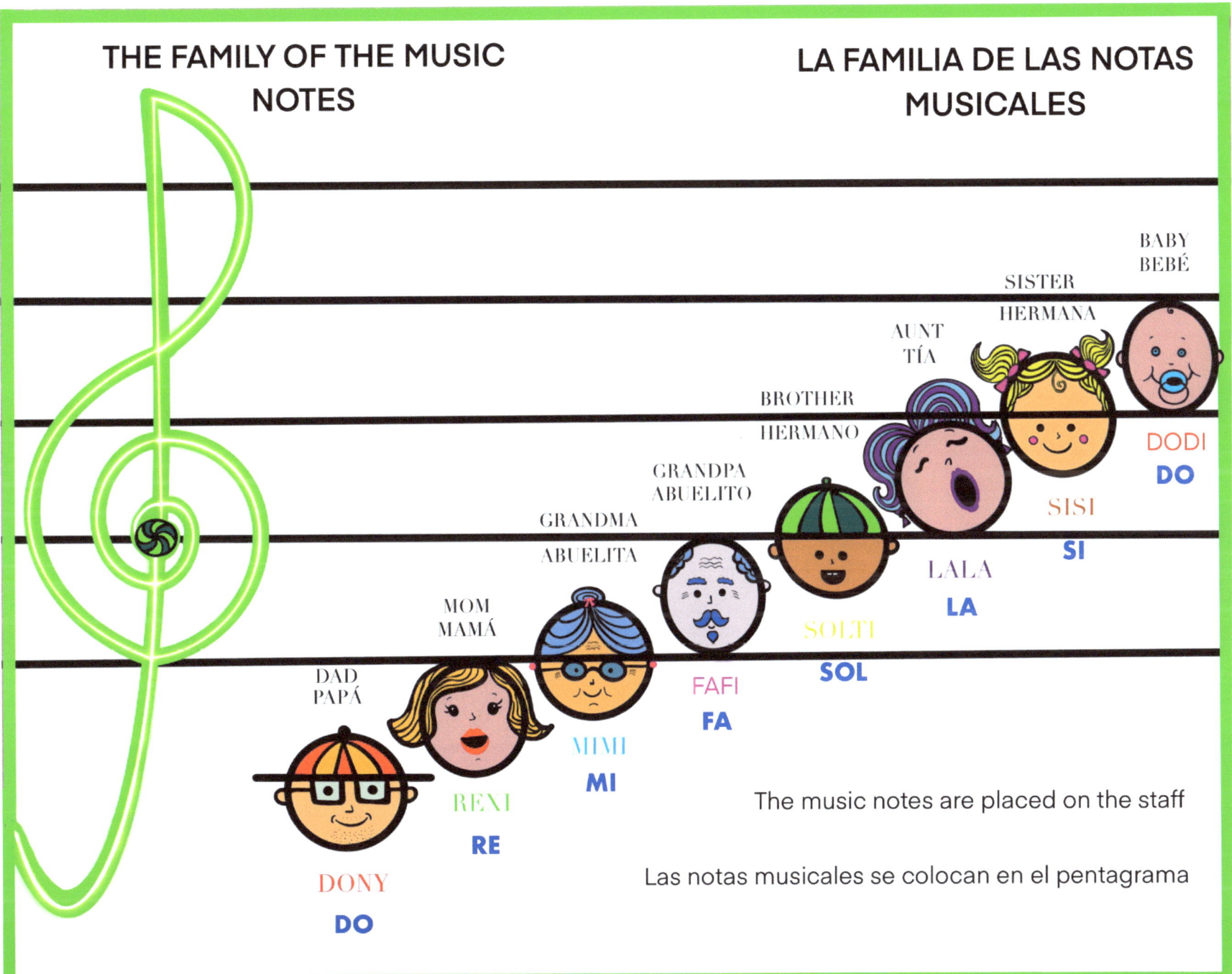

The music notes are placed on the staff

Las notas musicales se colocan en el pentagrama

Find who has a line in the middle of the head, who has a line above the head and who is in between the two lines

Encuentra quién tiene una línea en la mitad de la cabeza, quién tiene una línea encima de la cabeza y quién está en medio de las dos líneas

DONY

REXI

MIMI

FAFI

SOLTI

LALA

SISI

DODI

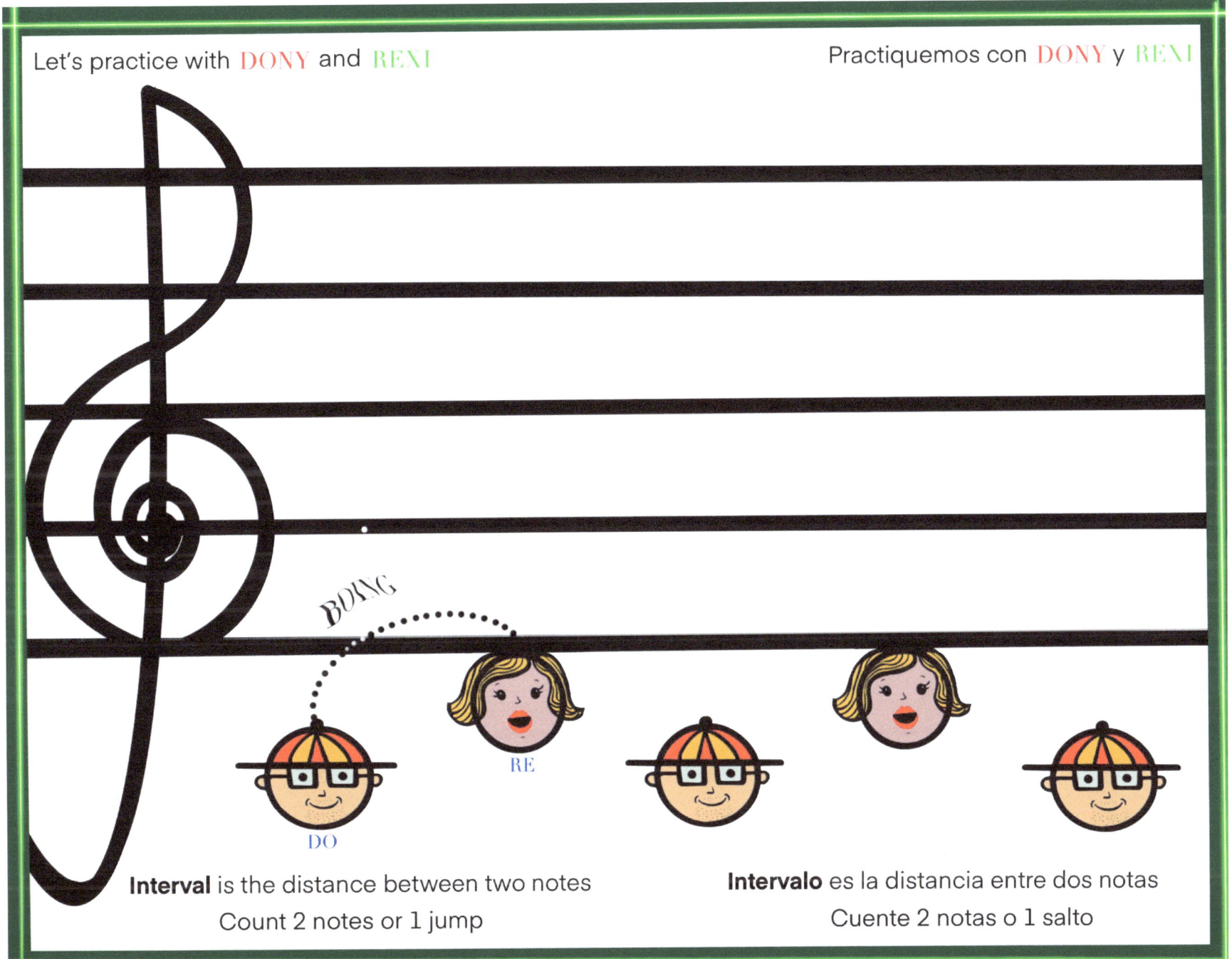

Interval is the distance between two notes

Count 2 notes or 1 jump

Intervalo es la distancia entre dos notas

Cuente 2 notas o 1 salto

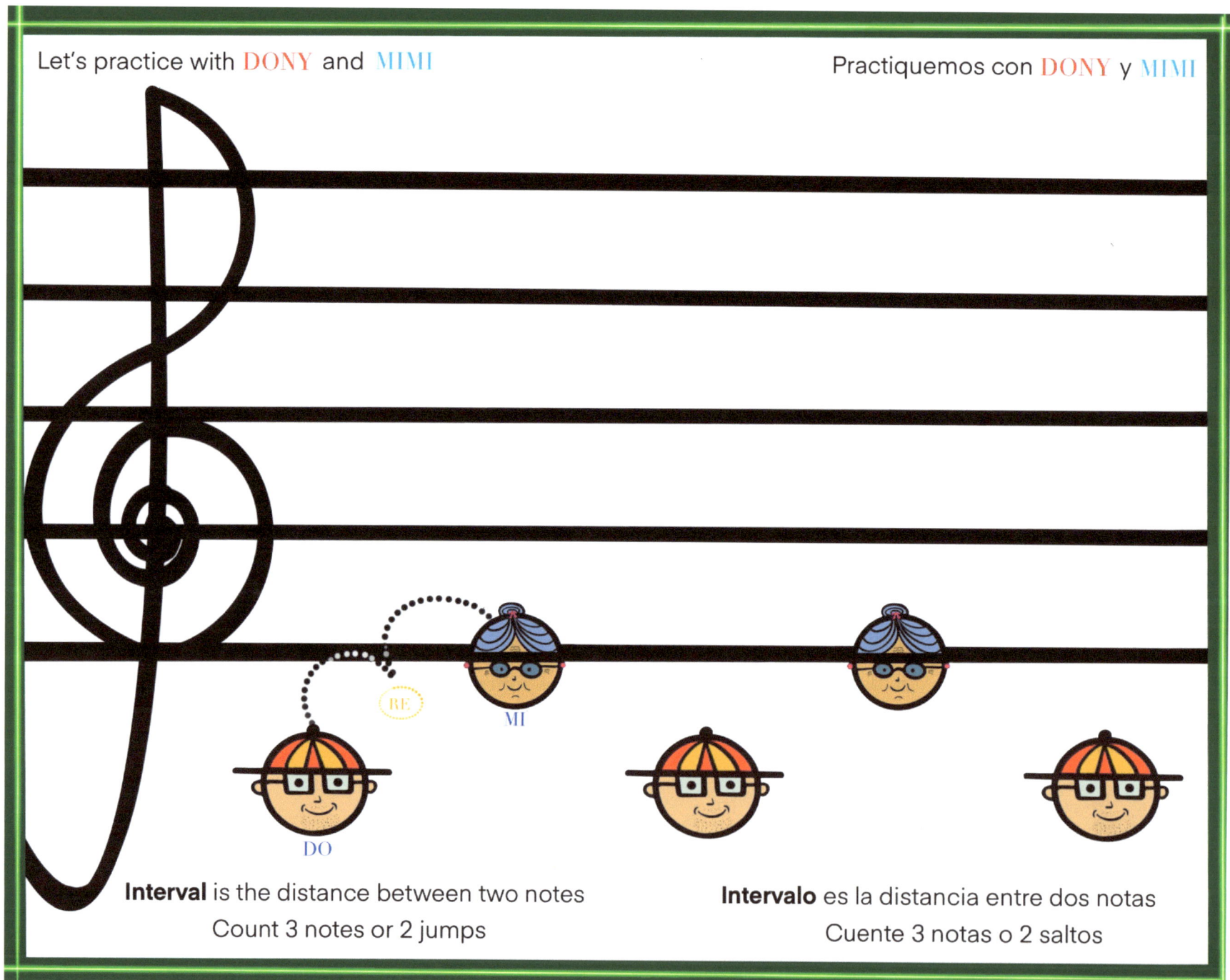

Interval is the distance between two notes
Count 3 notes or 2 jumps

Intervalo es la distancia entre dos notas
Cuente 3 notas o 2 saltos

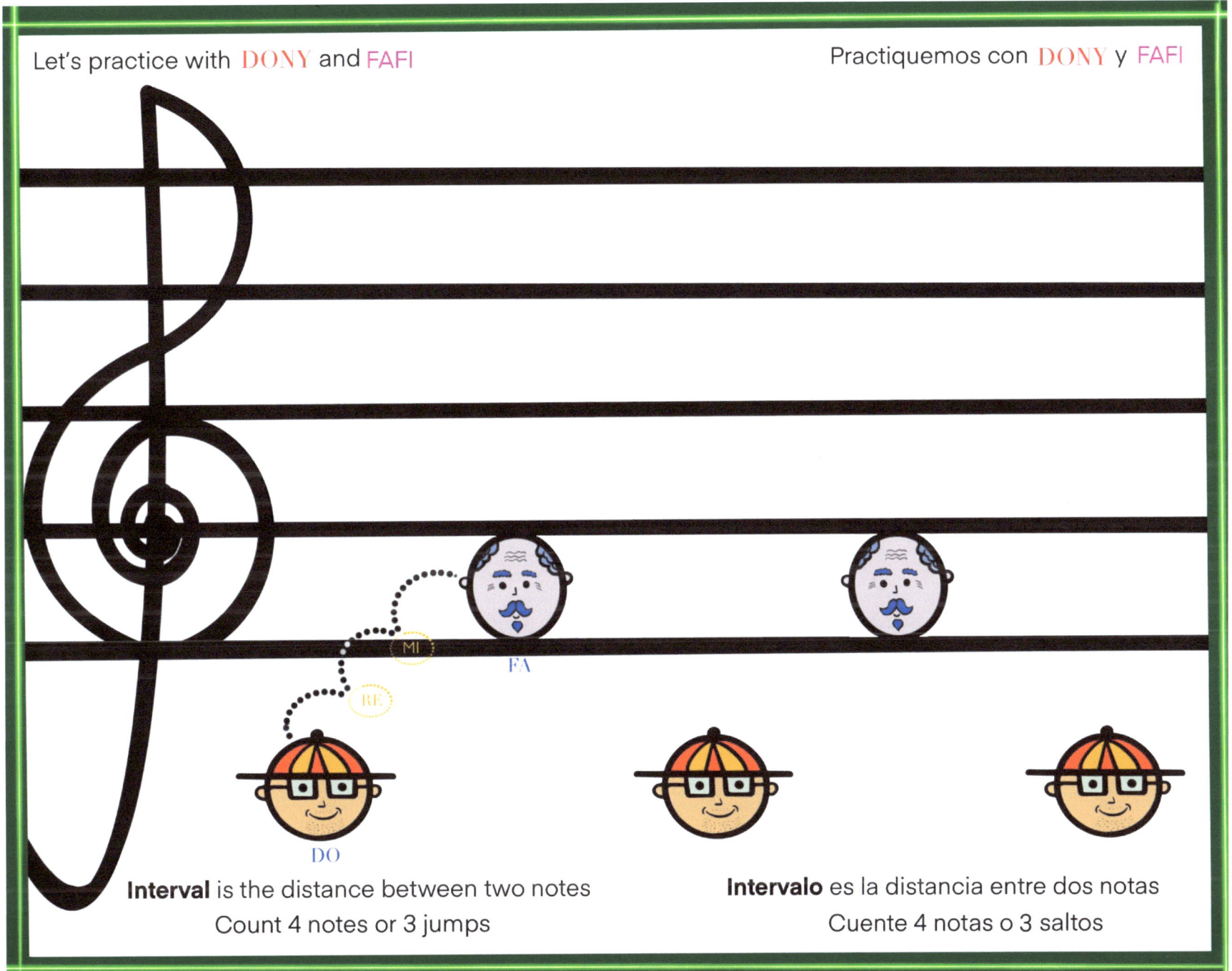

Interval is the distance between two notes
Count 4 notes or 3 jumps

Intervalo es la distancia entre dos notas
Cuente 4 notas o 3 saltos

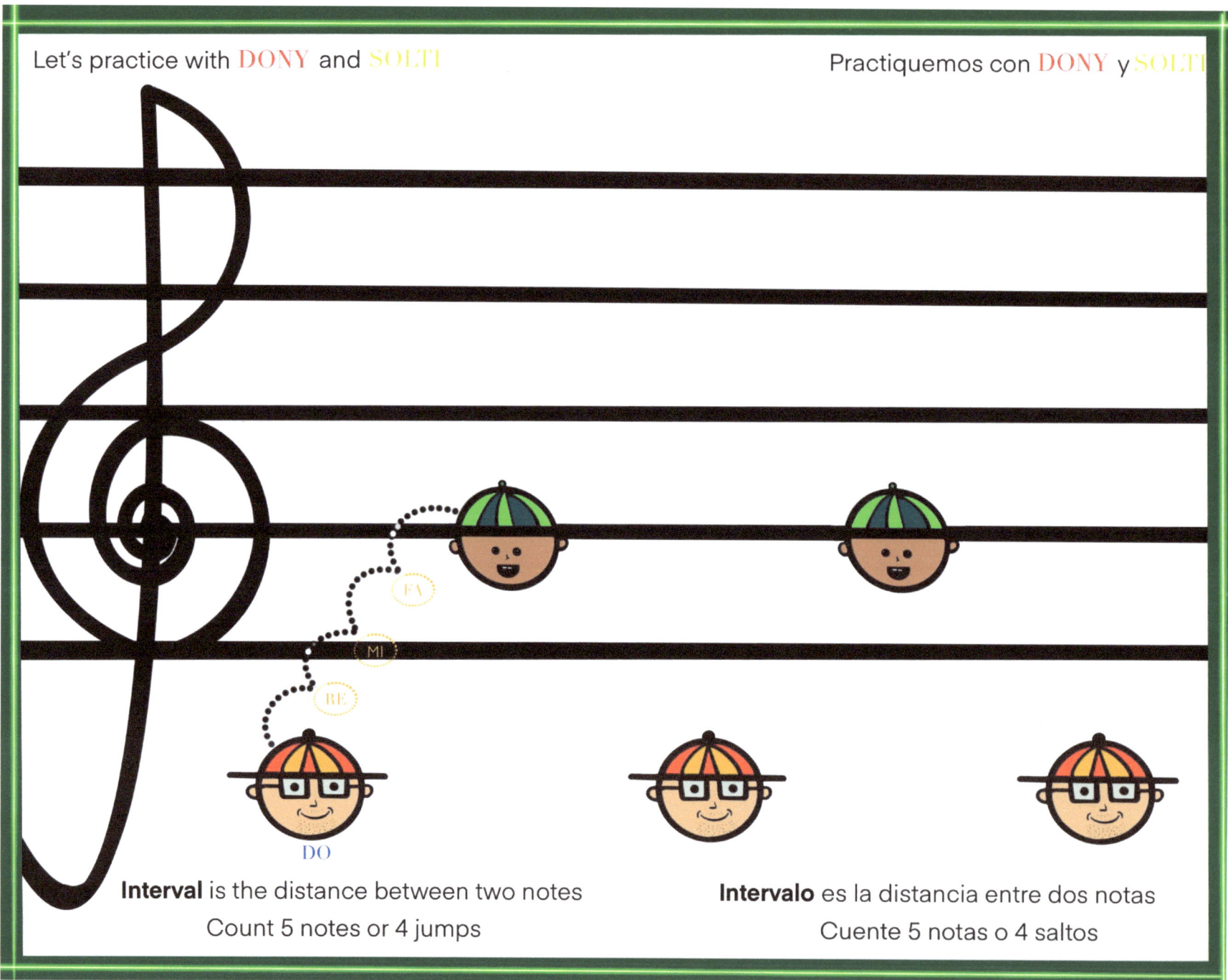

Interval is the distance between two notes

Count 5 notes or 4 jumps

Intervalo es la distancia entre dos notas

Cuente 5 notas o 4 saltos

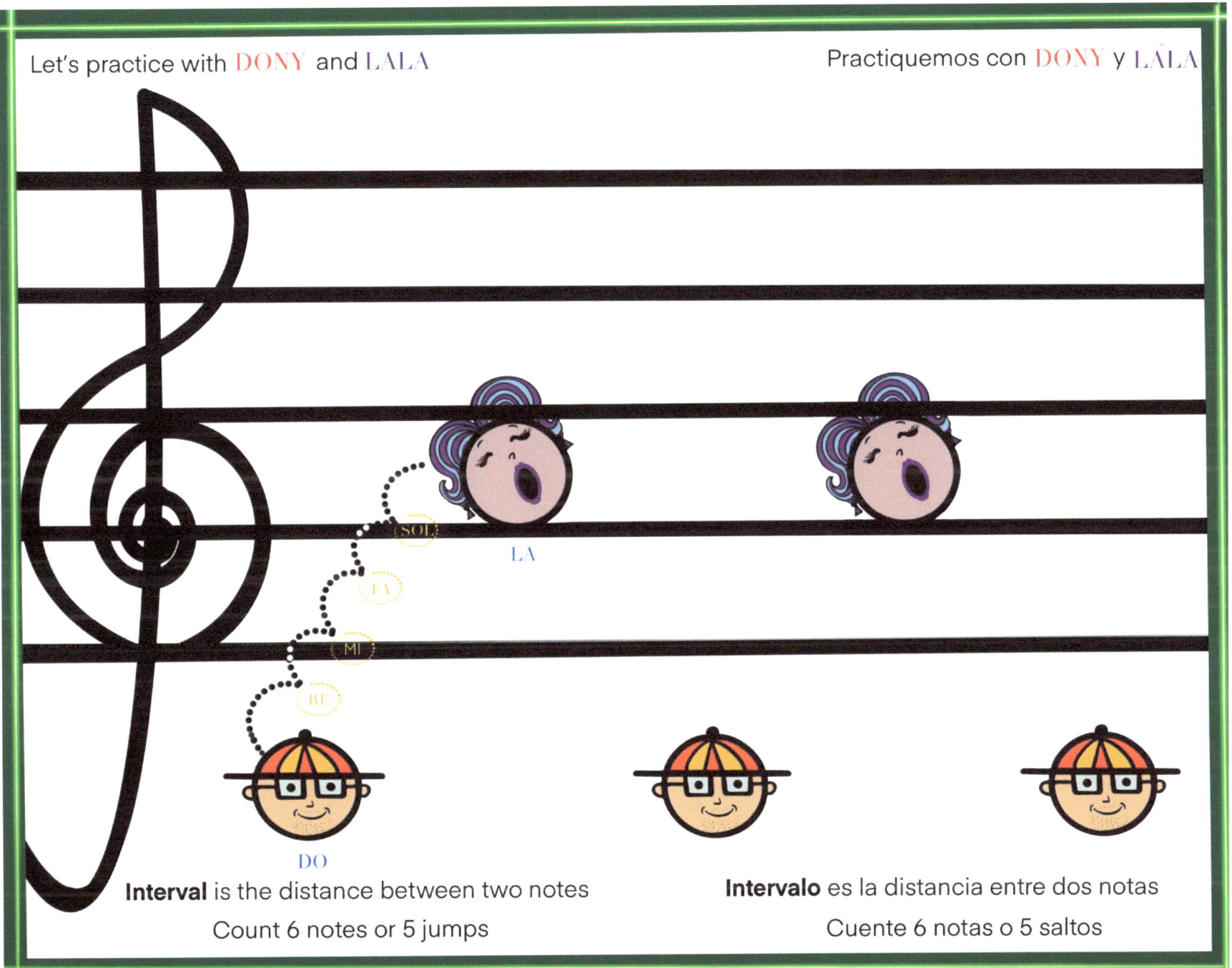

Interval is the distance between two notes

Count 6 notes or 5 jumps

Intervalo es la distancia entre dos notas

Cuente 6 notas o 5 saltos

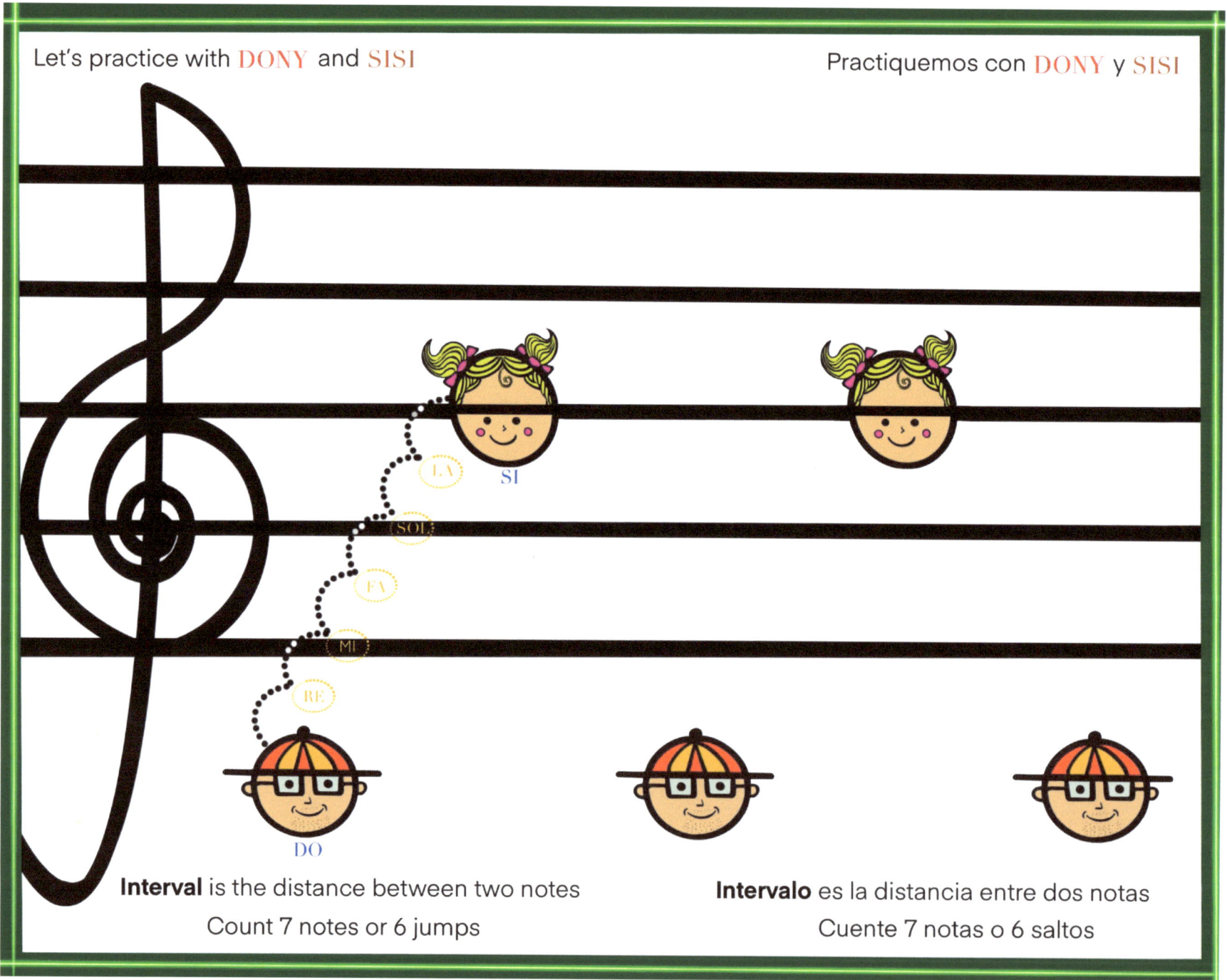

Interval is the distance between two notes

Count 7 notes or 6 jumps

Intervalo es la distancia entre dos notas

Cuente 7 notas o 6 saltos

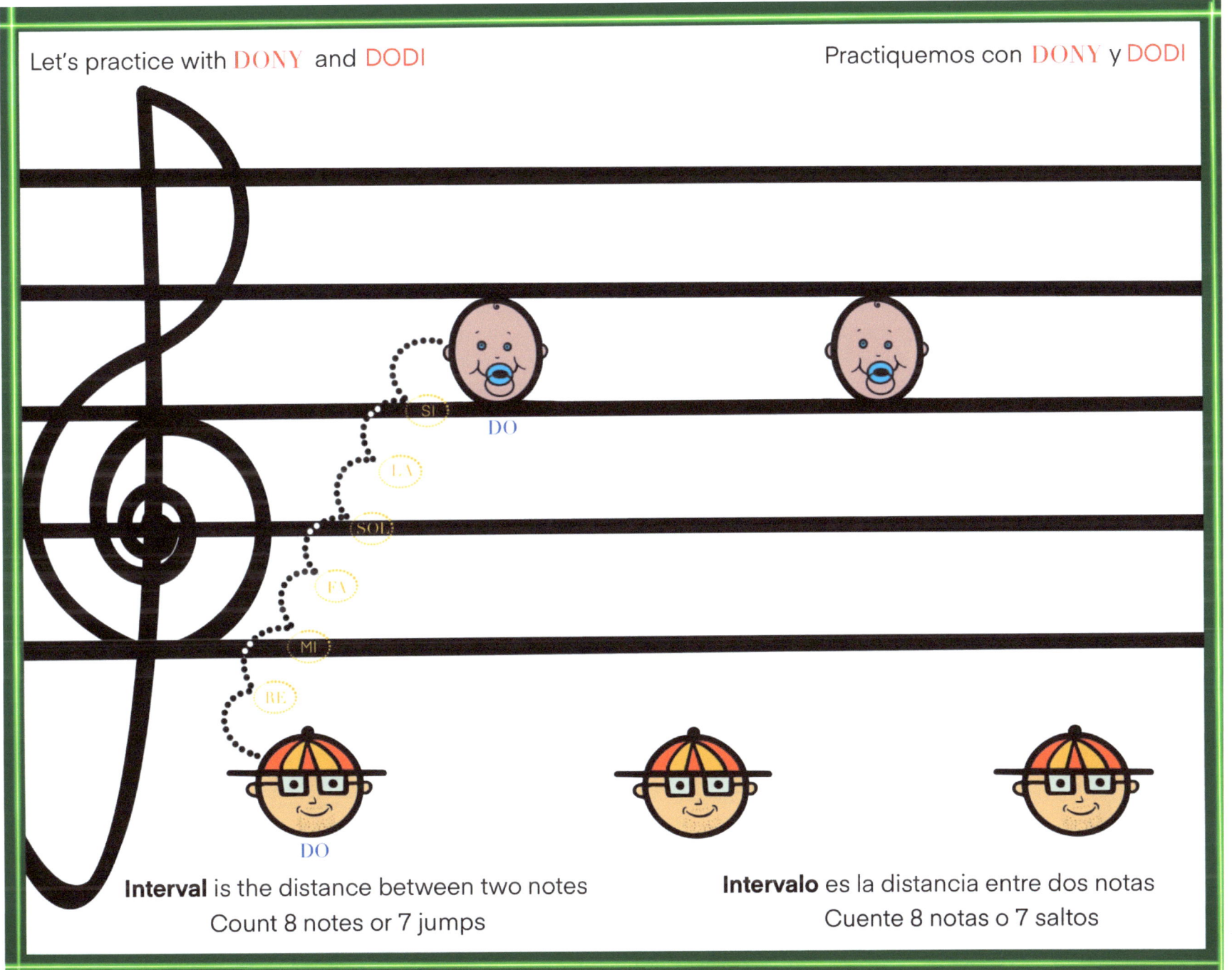

Interval is the distance between two notes
Count 8 notes or 7 jumps

Intervalo es la distancia entre dos notas
Cuente 8 notas o 7 saltos

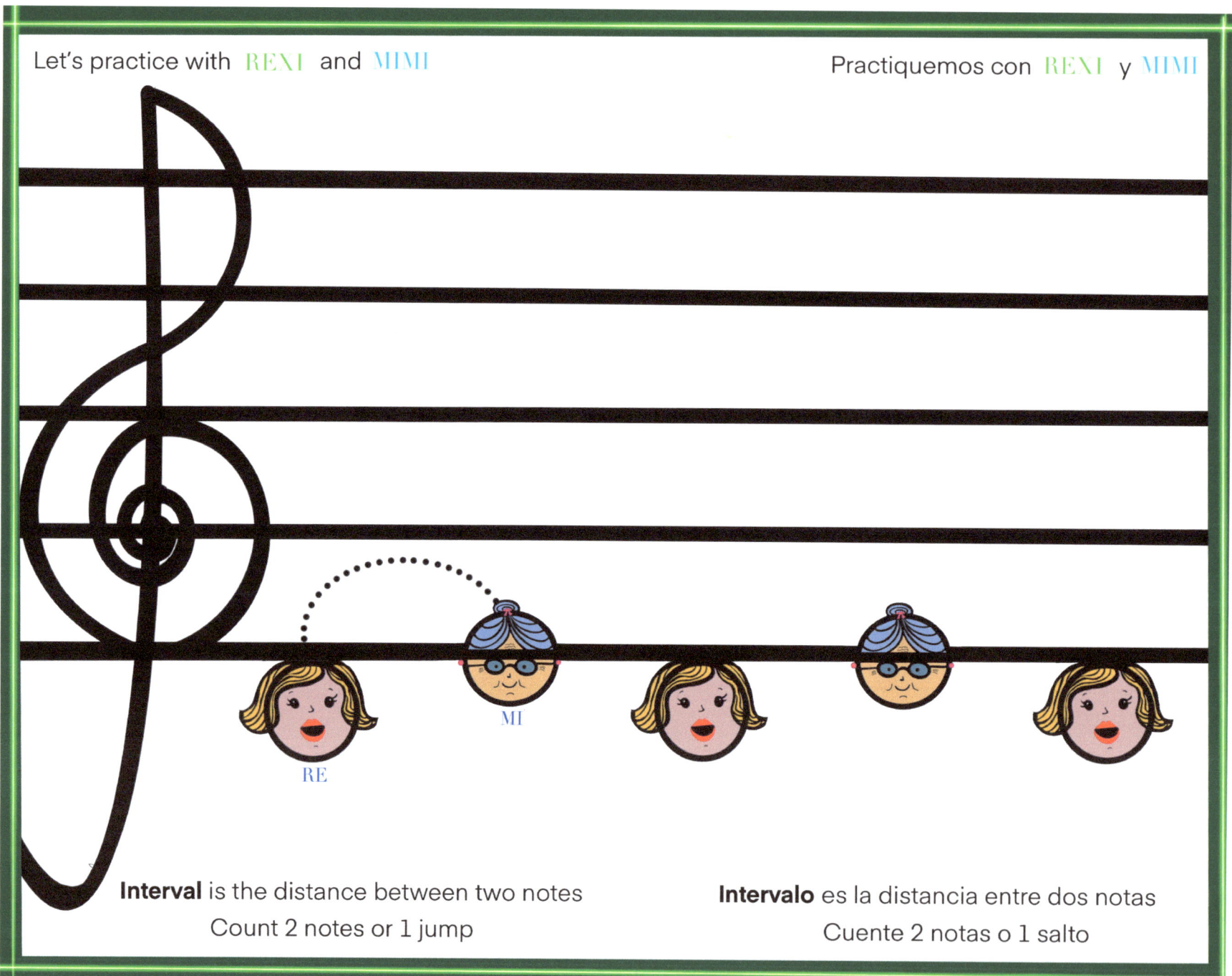

Interval is the distance between two notes
Count 2 notes or 1 jump

Intervalo es la distancia entre dos notas
Cuente 2 notas o 1 salto

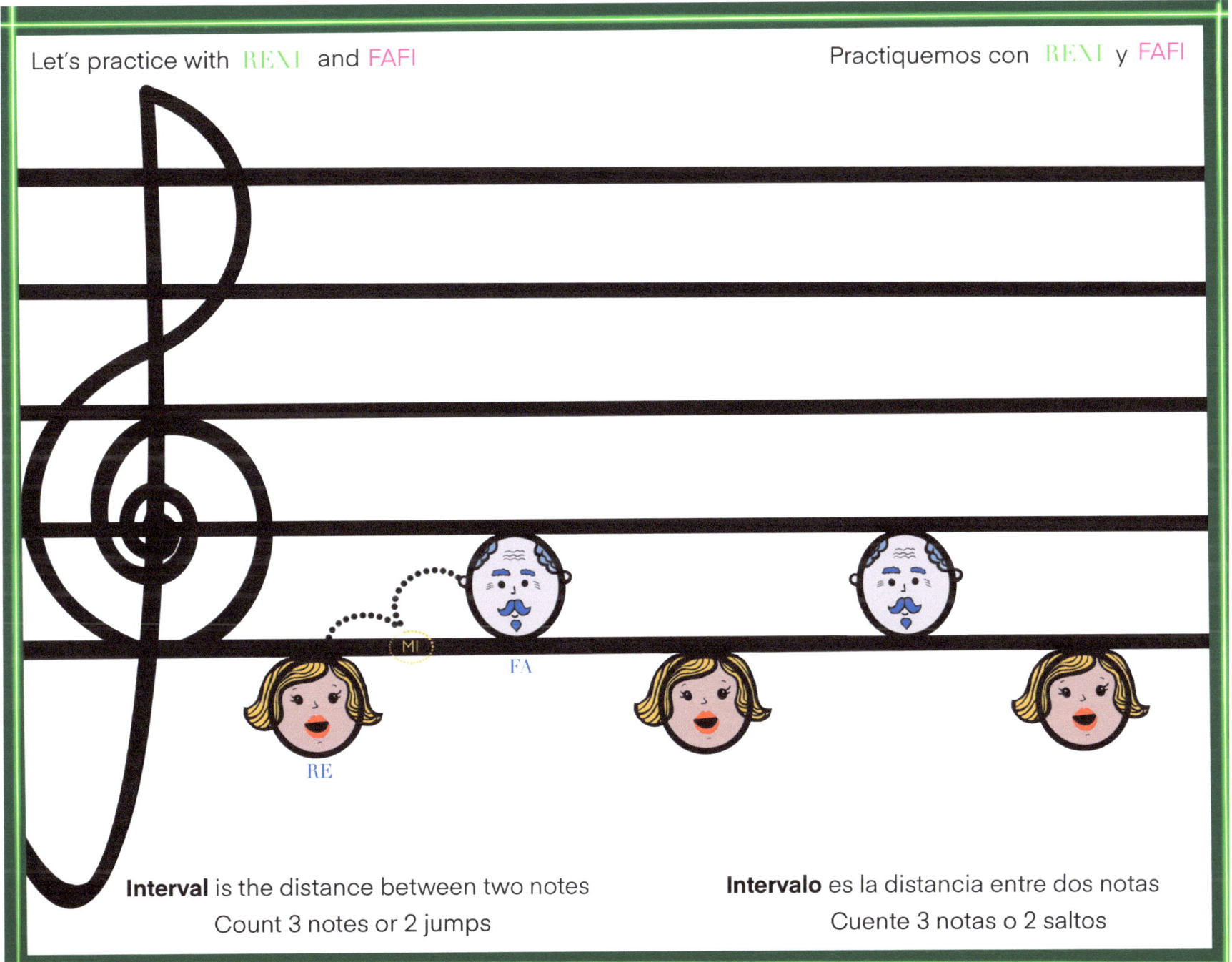

Interval is the distance between two notes
Count 3 notes or 2 jumps

Intervalo es la distancia entre dos notas
Cuente 3 notas o 2 saltos

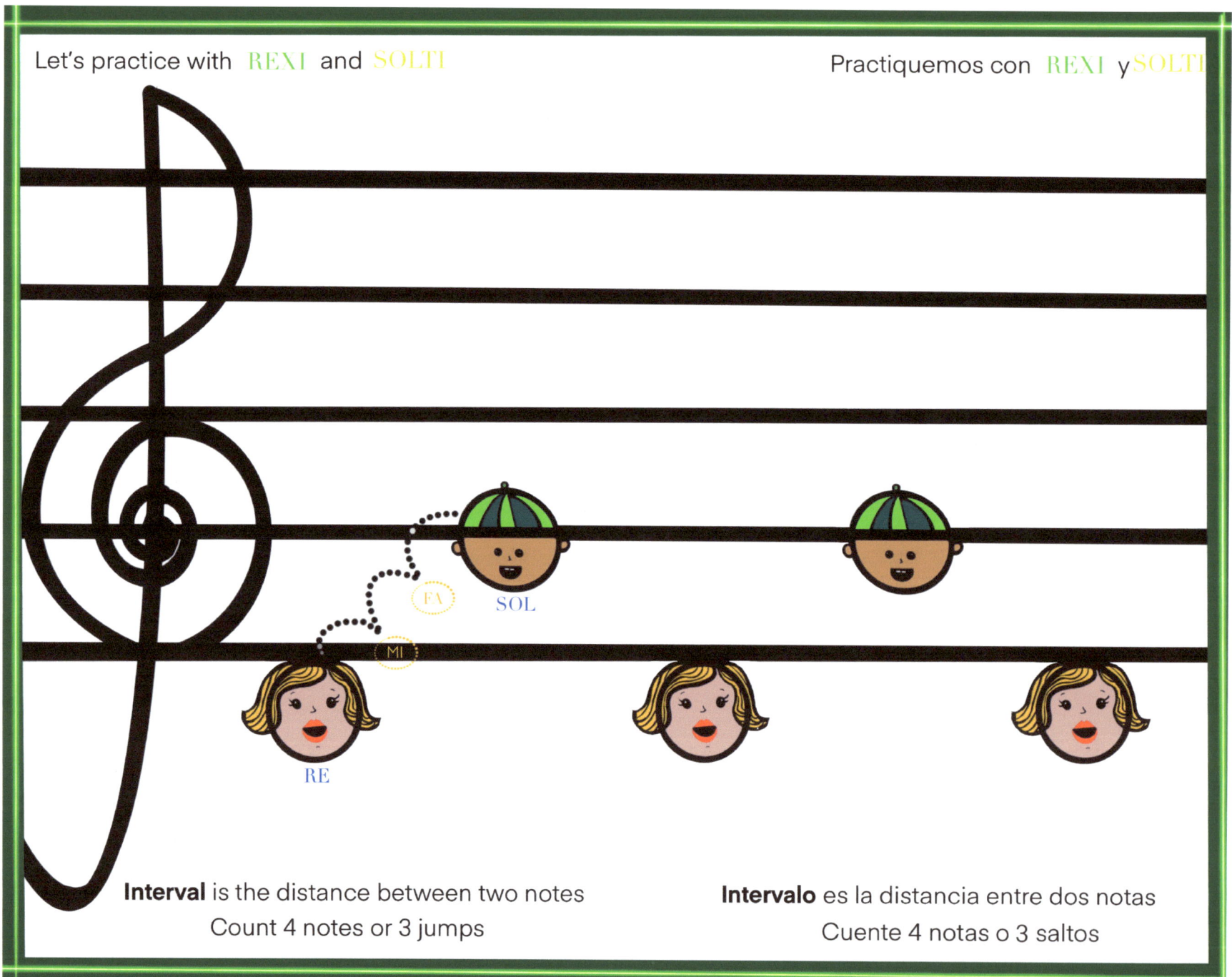

Interval is the distance between two notes
Count 4 notes or 3 jumps

Intervalo es la distancia entre dos notas
Cuente 4 notas o 3 saltos

Interval is the distance between two notes
Count 5 notes or 4 jumps

Intervalo es la distancia entre dos notas
Cuente 5 notas o 4 saltos

Interval is the distance between two notes

Count 6 notes or 5 jumps

Intervalo es la distancia entre dos notas

Cuente 6 notas o 5 saltos

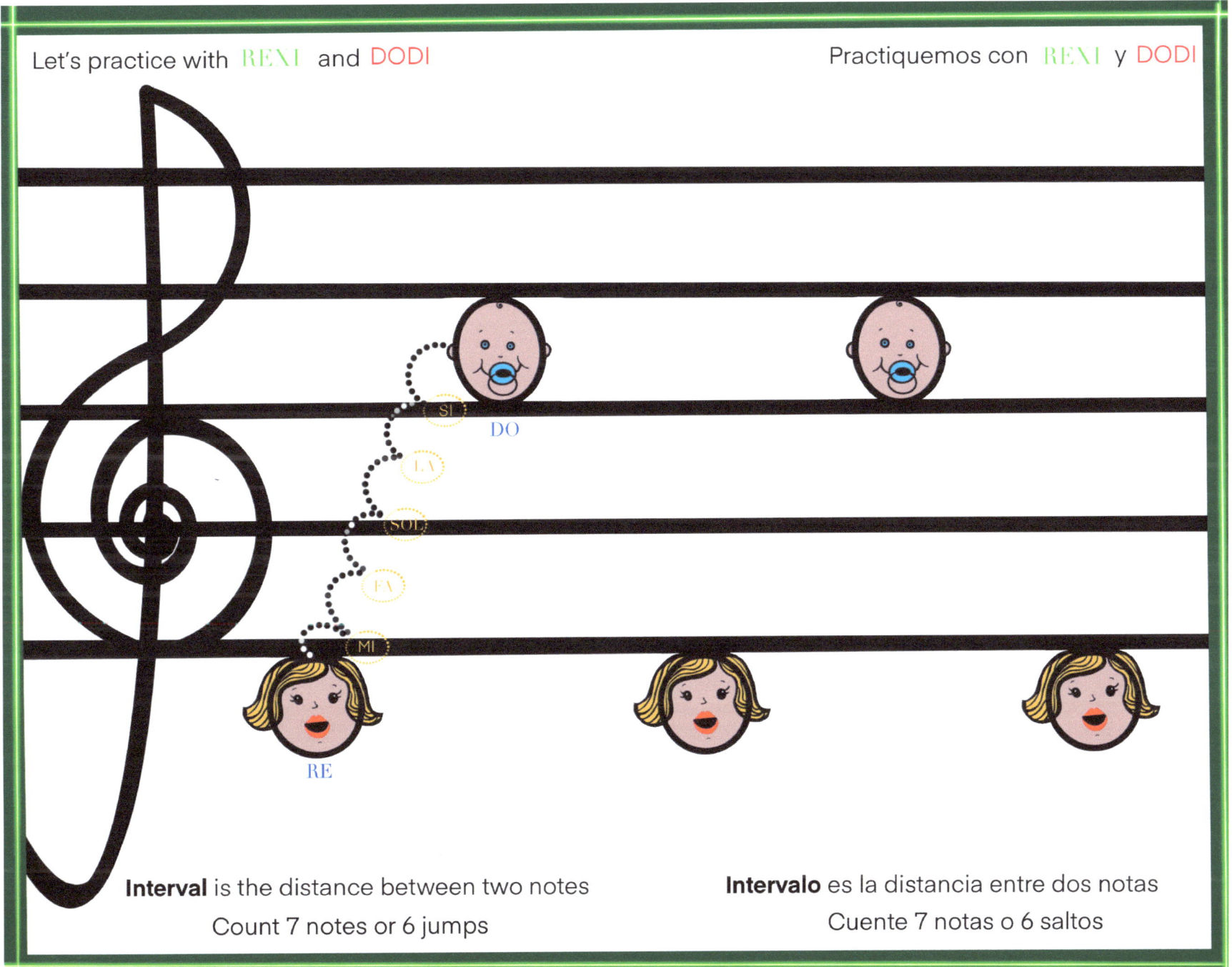

Interval is the distance between two notes

Count 7 notes or 6 jumps

Intervalo es la distancia entre dos notas

Cuente 7 notas o 6 saltos

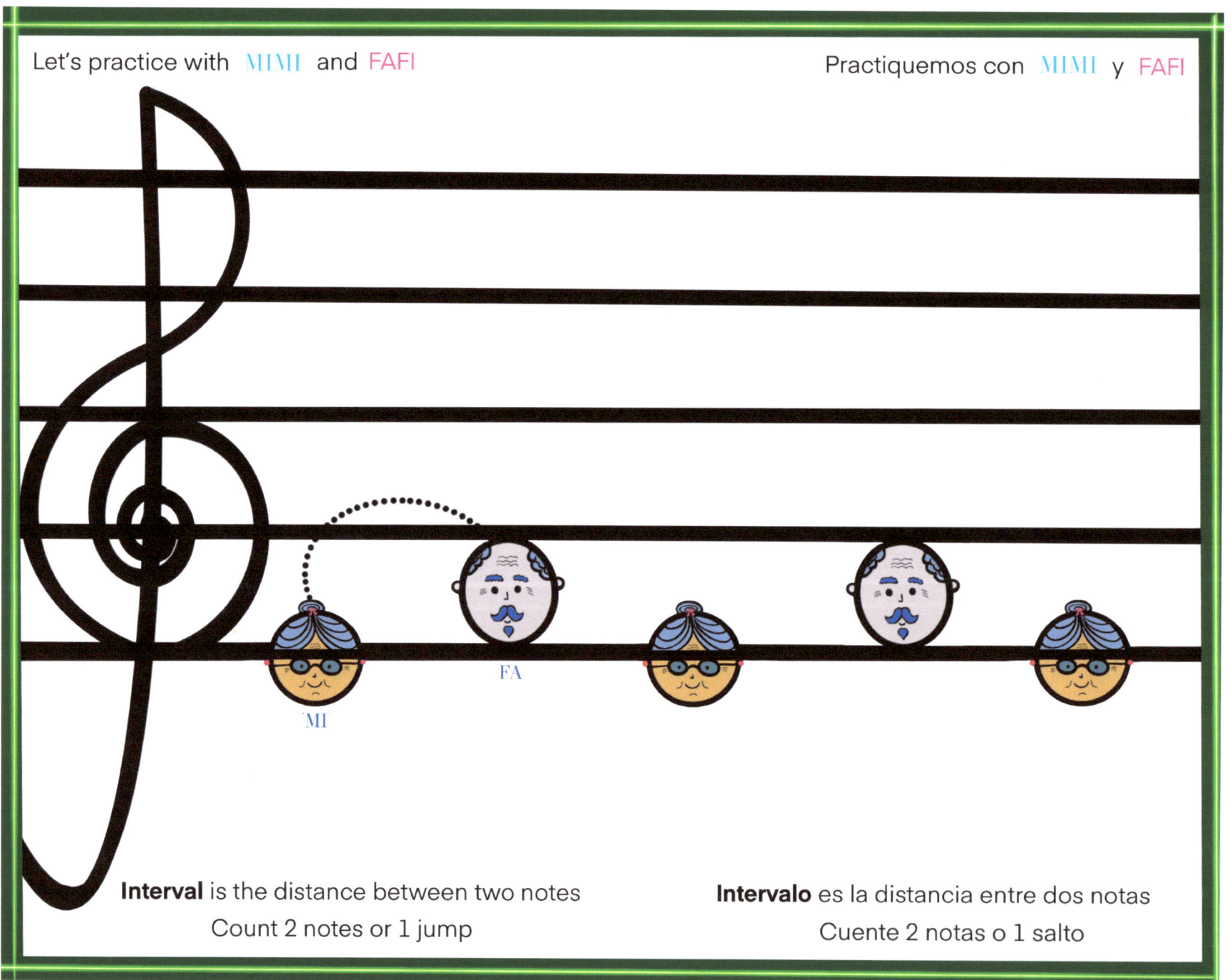

Interval is the distance between two notes

Count 2 notes or 1 jump

Intervalo es la distancia entre dos notas

Cuente 2 notas o 1 salto

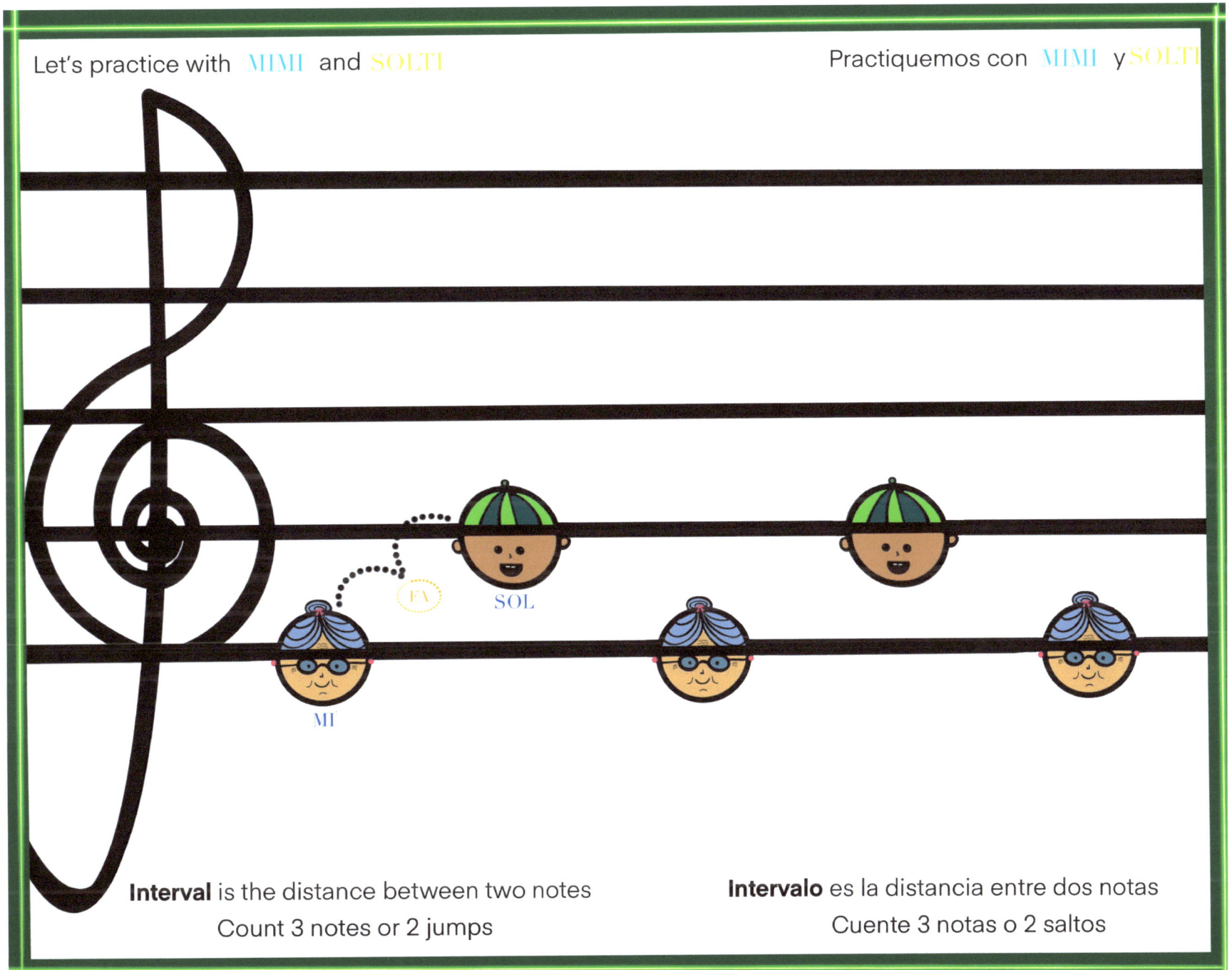

Interval is the distance between two notes

Count 3 notes or 2 jumps

Intervalo es la distancia entre dos notas

Cuente 3 notas o 2 saltos

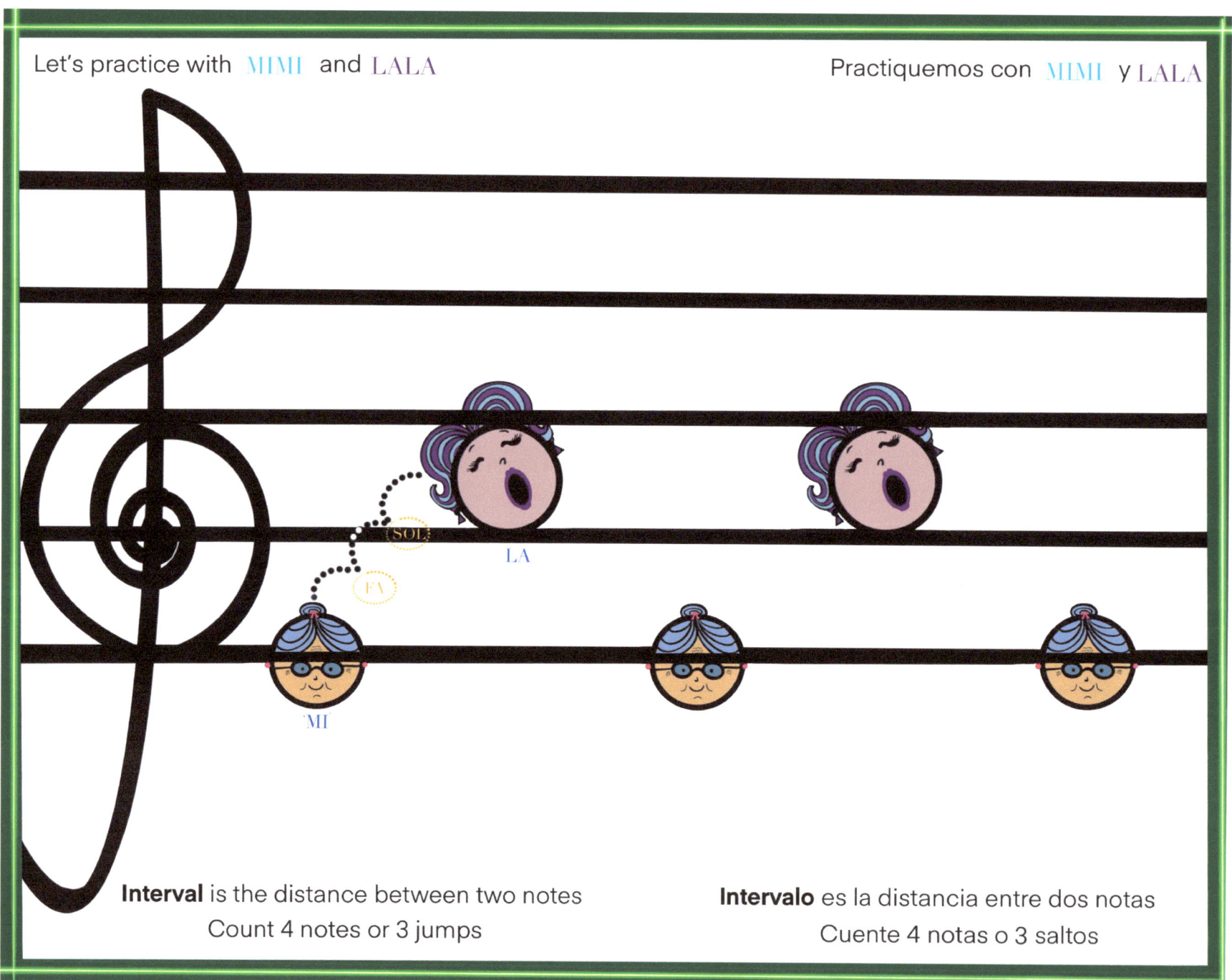

Interval is the distance between two notes
Count 4 notes or 3 jumps

Intervalo es la distancia entre dos notas
Cuente 4 notas o 3 saltos

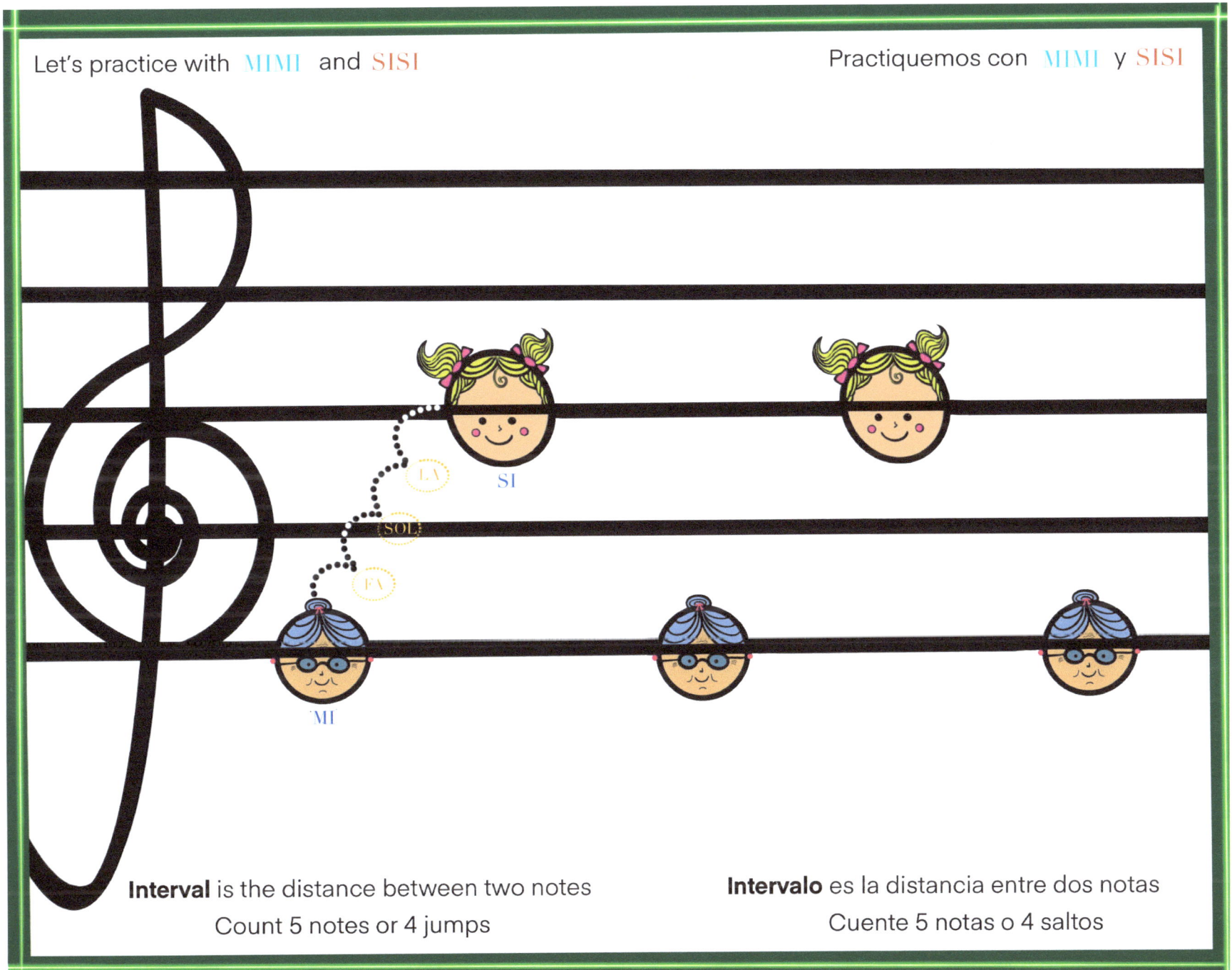

Interval is the distance between two notes

Count 5 notes or 4 jumps

Intervalo es la distancia entre dos notas

Cuente 5 notas o 4 saltos

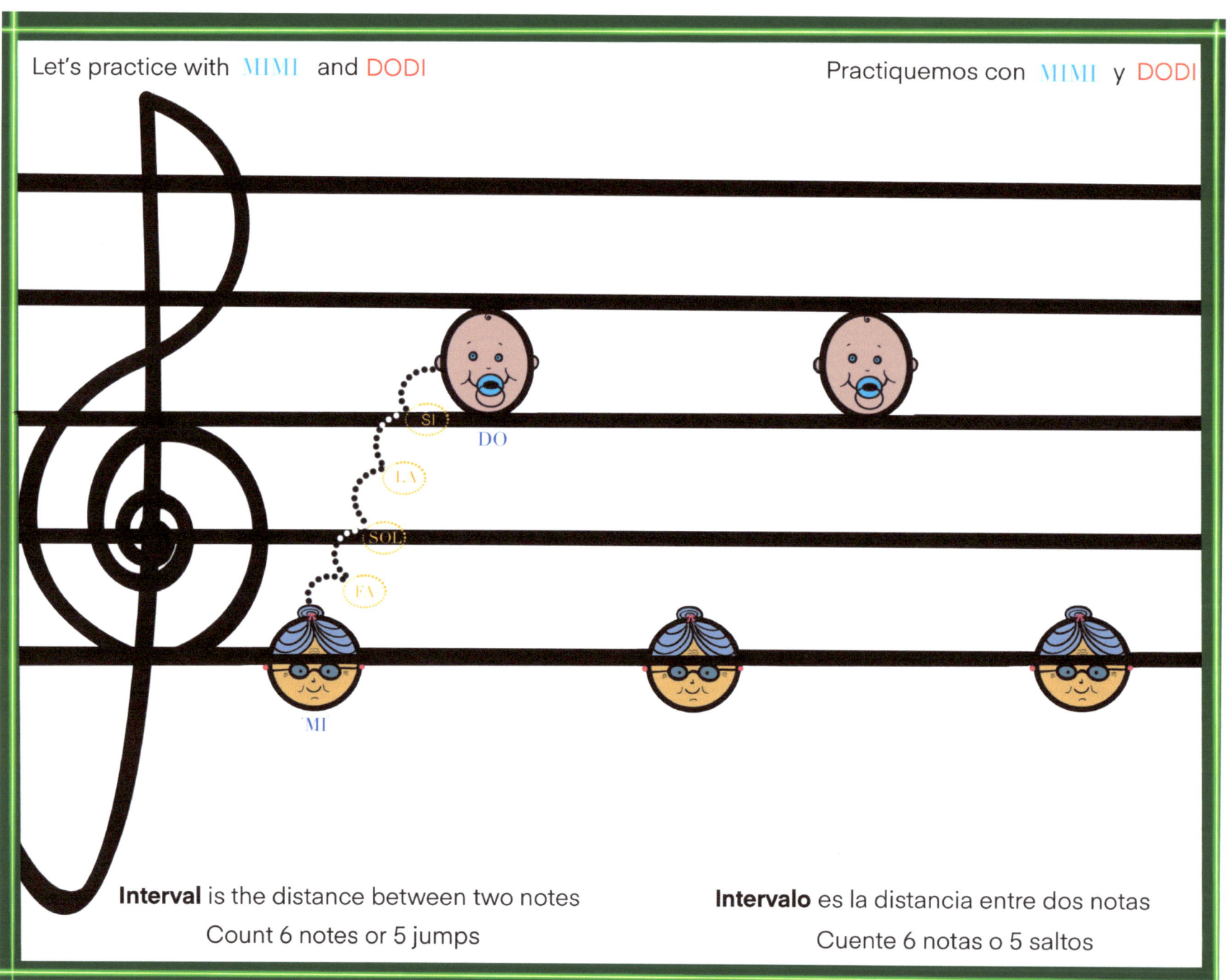

Interval is the distance between two notes
Count 6 notes or 5 jumps

Intervalo es la distancia entre dos notas
Cuente 6 notas o 5 saltos

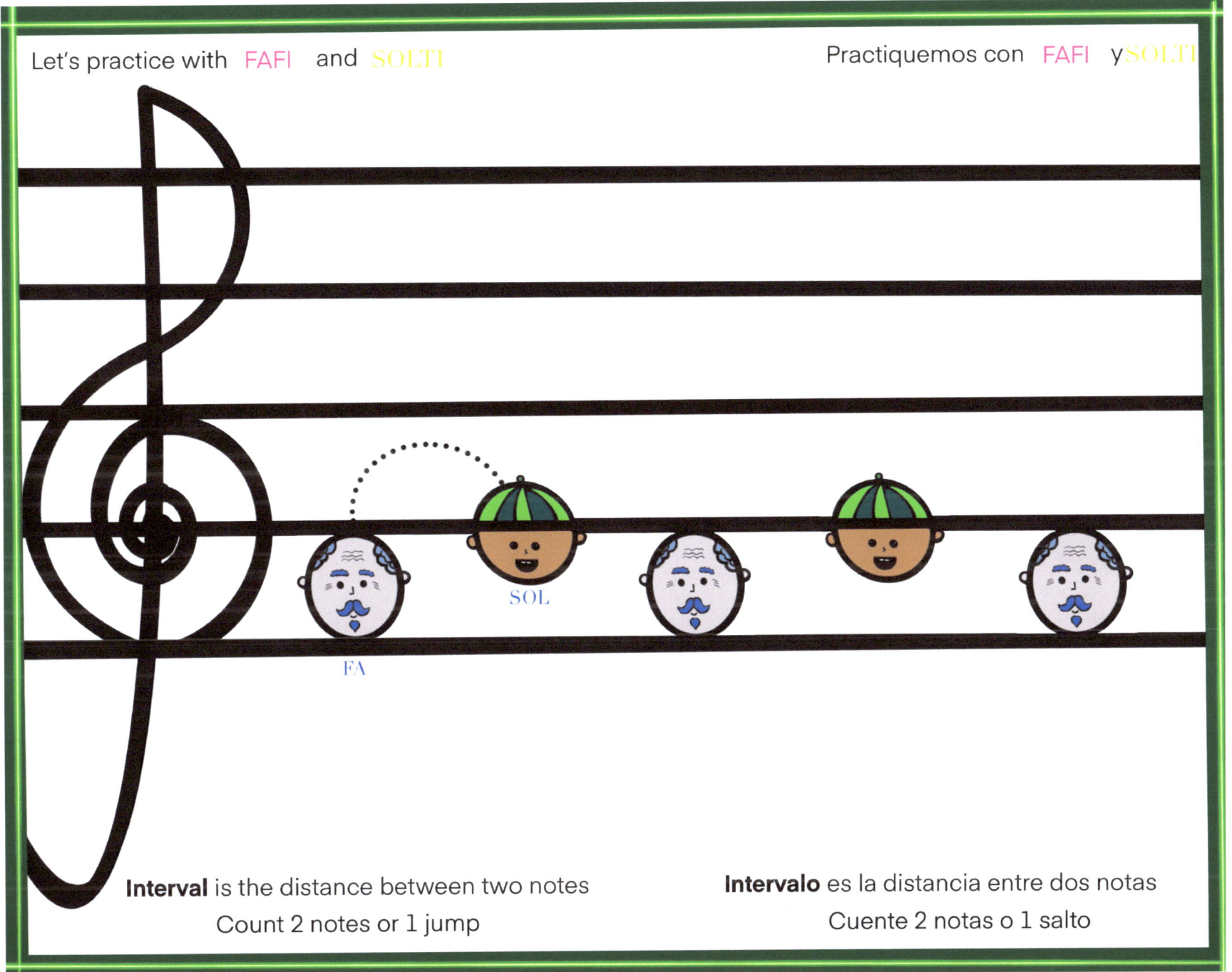

Interval is the distance between two notes
Count 2 notes or 1 jump

Intervalo es la distancia entre dos notas
Cuente 2 notas o 1 salto

Interval is the distance between two notes

Count 3 notes or 2 jumps

Intervalo es la distancia entre dos notas

Cuente 3 notas o 2 saltos

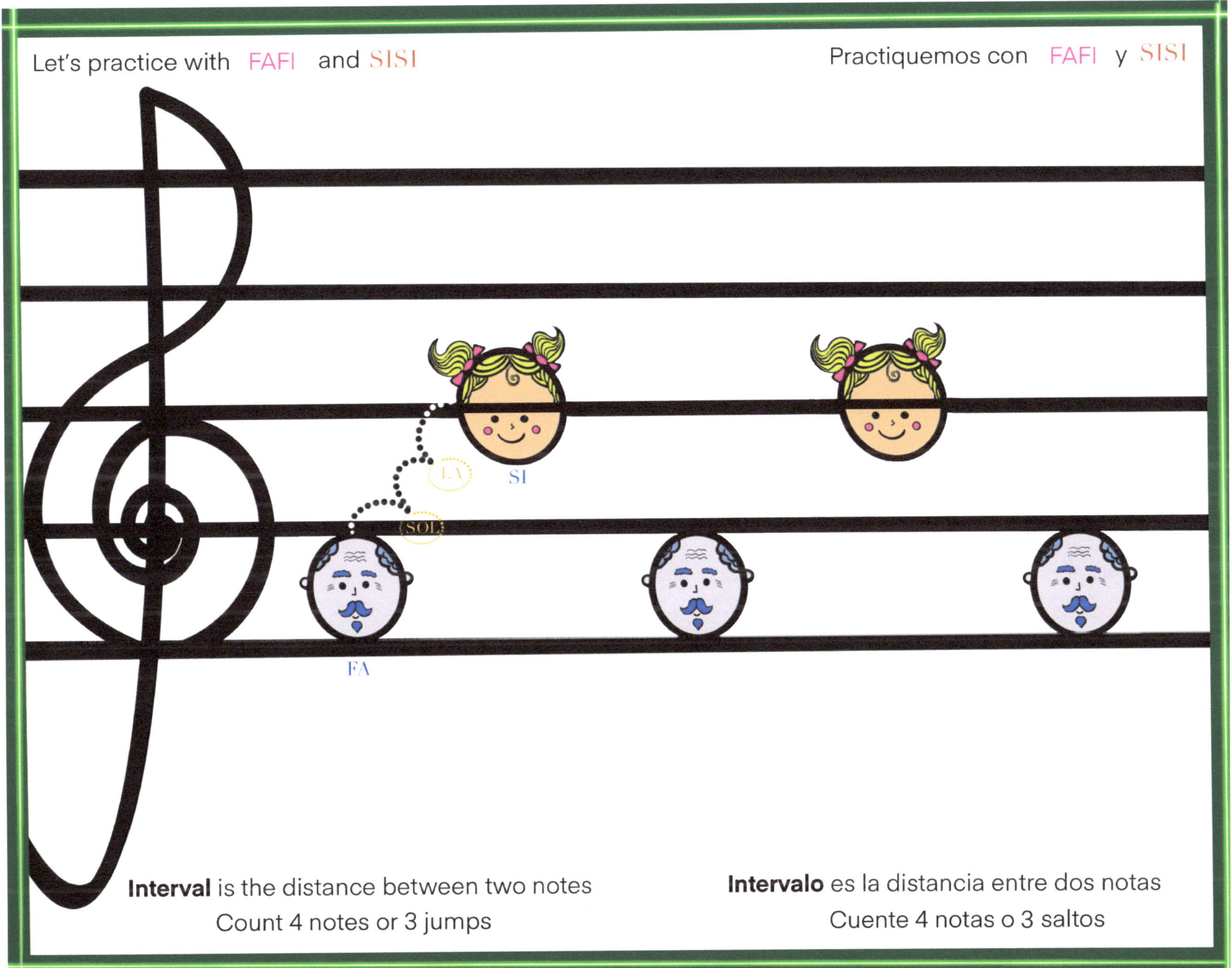

Interval is the distance between two notes
Count 4 notes or 3 jumps

Intervalo es la distancia entre dos notas
Cuente 4 notas o 3 saltos

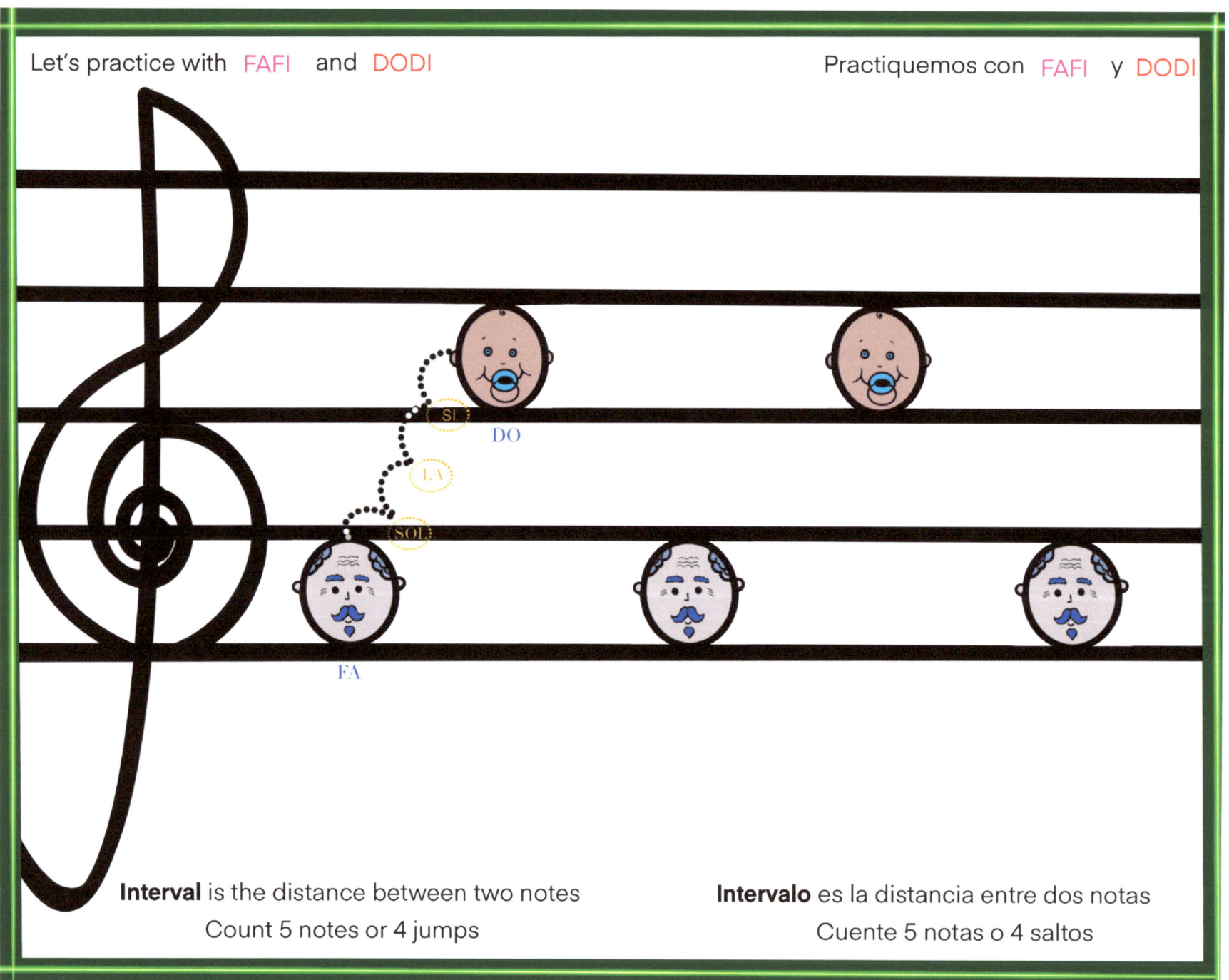

Interval is the distance between two notes

Count 5 notes or 4 jumps

Intervalo es la distancia entre dos notas

Cuente 5 notas o 4 saltos

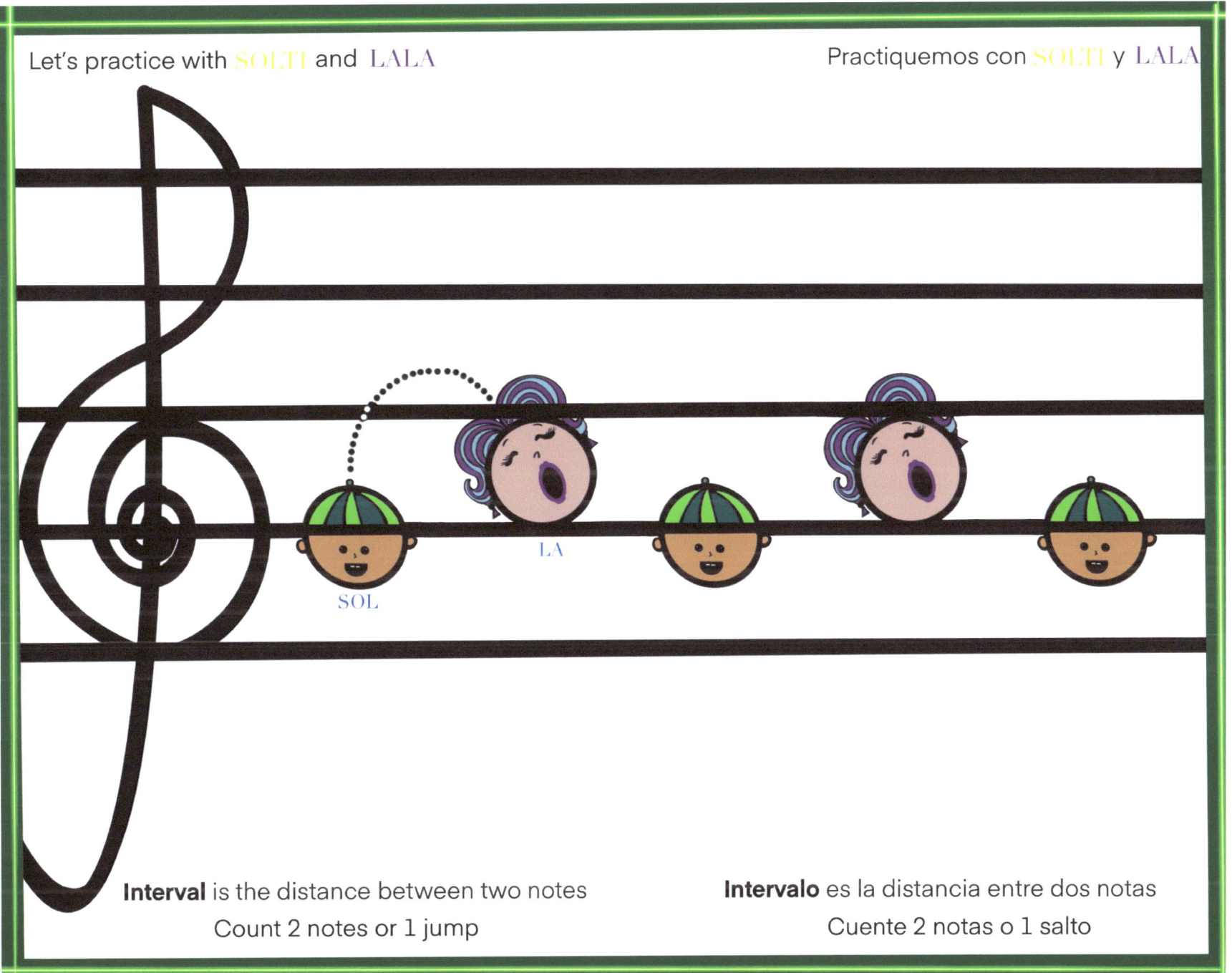

Interval is the distance between two notes

Count 2 notes or 1 jump

Intervalo es la distancia entre dos notas

Cuente 2 notas o 1 salto

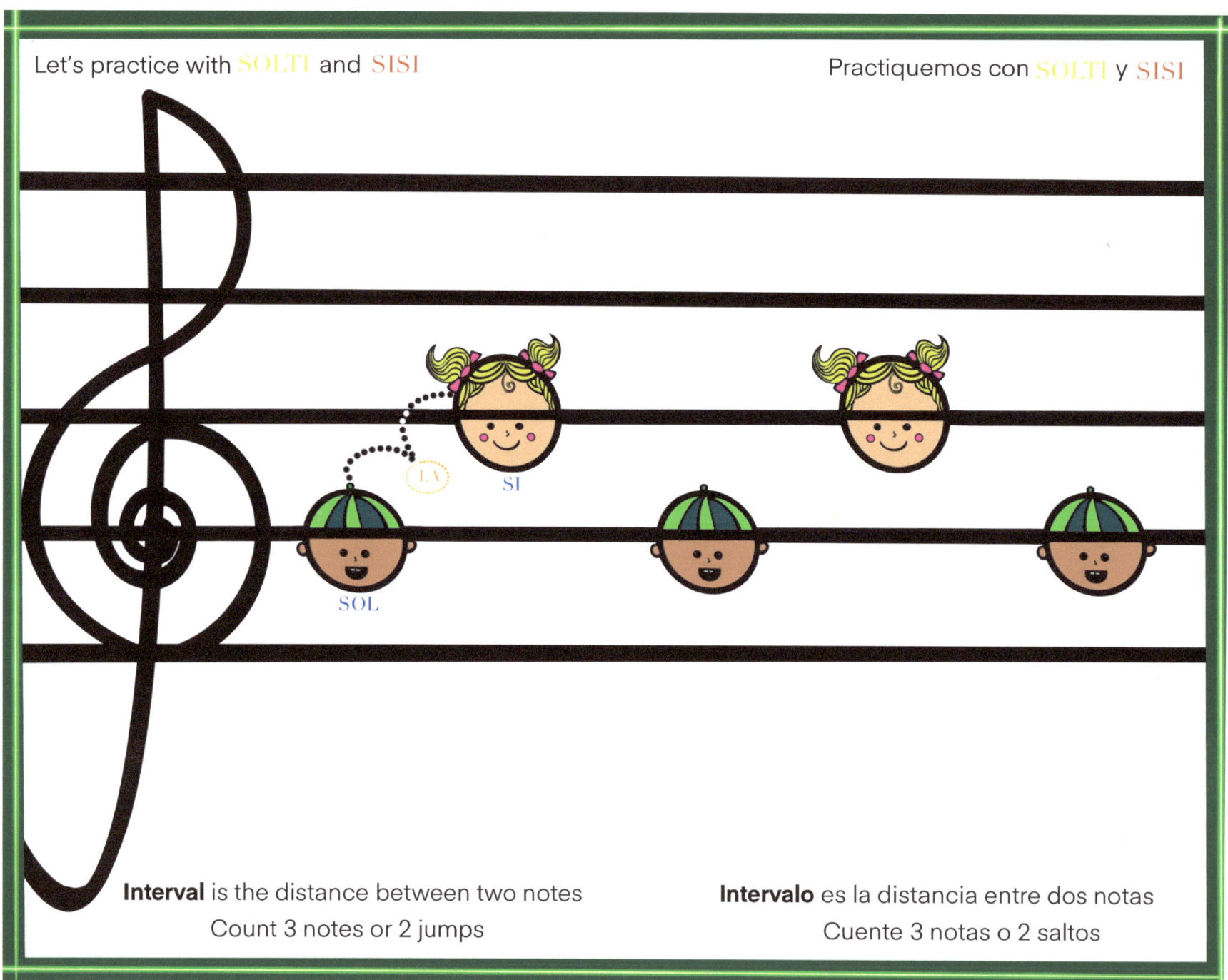

Interval is the distance between two notes

Count 3 notes or 2 jumps

Intervalo es la distancia entre dos notas

Cuente 3 notas o 2 saltos

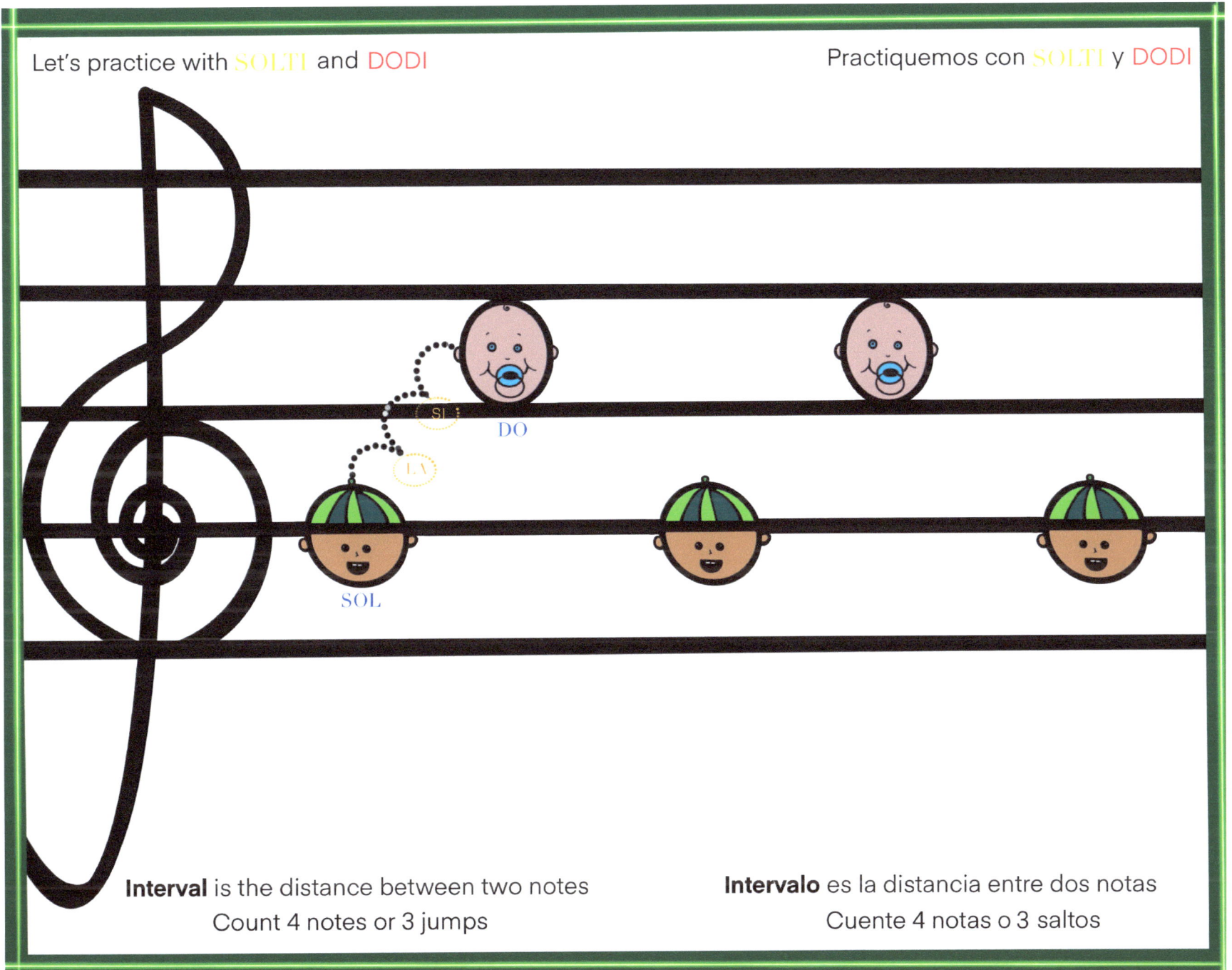

Interval is the distance between two notes
Count 4 notes or 3 jumps

Intervalo es la distancia entre dos notas
Cuente 4 notas o 3 saltos

Interval is the distance between two notes
Count 2 notes or 1 jump

Intervalo es la distancia entre dos notas
Cuente 2 notas o 1 salto

Interval is the distance between two notes
Count 3 notes or 2 jumps

Intervalo es la distancia entre dos notas
Cuente 3 notas o 2 saltos

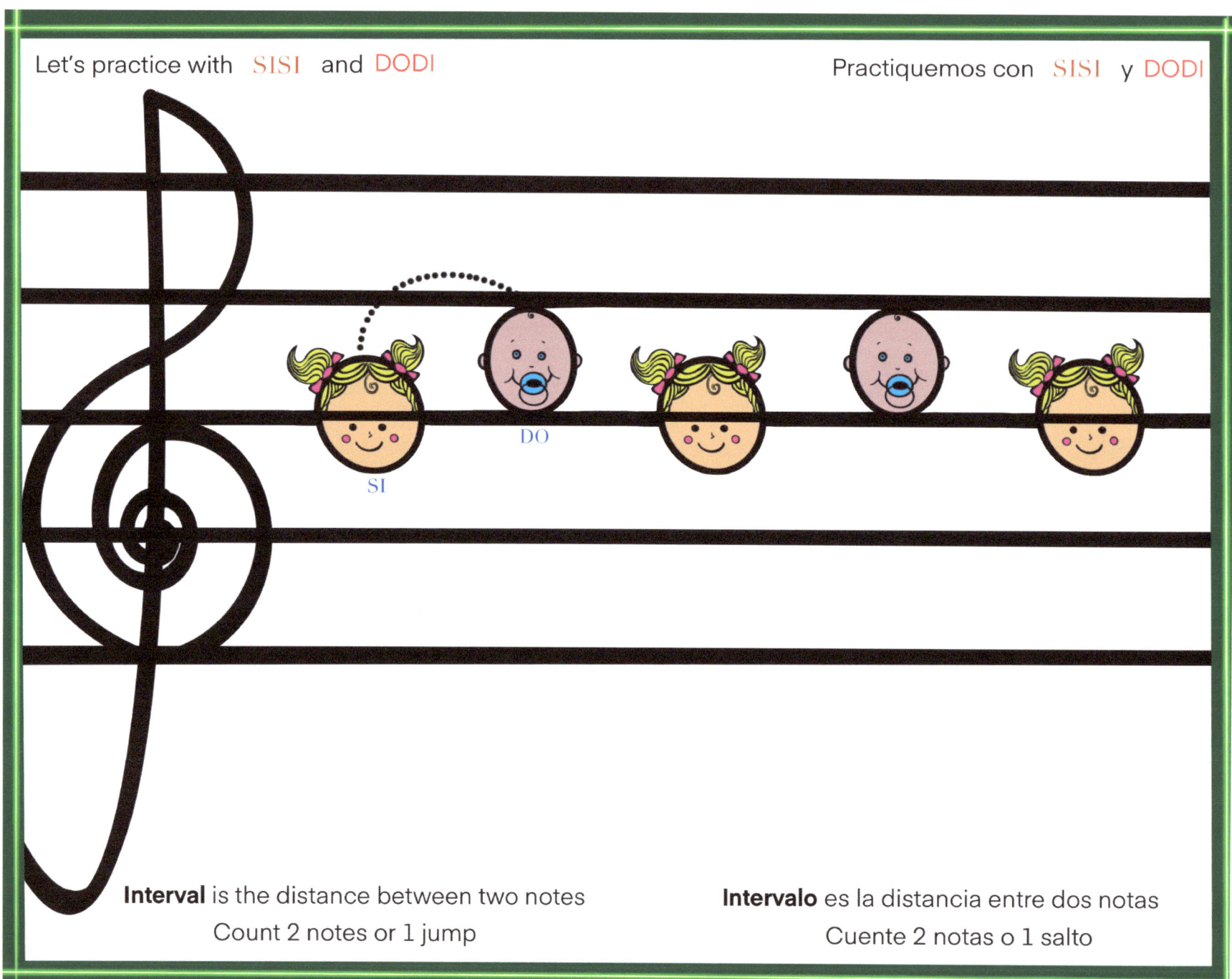

Interval is the distance between two notes

Count 2 notes or 1 jump

Intervalo es la distancia entre dos notas

Cuente 2 notas o 1 salto

AUTHOR'S BIOGRAPHY – BIOGRAFÍA DE LA AUTORA

Rocío Rodríguez is a professional harpist and has been part of numerous symphony orchestras in Canada, United States, Sweden, Spain, Colombia, and Arab Emirates. In addition, she has been interested in teaching music to children and for more than 20 years she has taught music with private classes and in different educational and musical institutions. Through her enormous experience, Rocío has designed a unique musical learning system for preschoolers so children can quickly learn music reading in a fun way that will serve as the basis to start playing any musical instrument. This system based on different methods such as Kodaly, Montessori, the French system (solfège or solfeggio) and the English system (letters notes) is reflected in **The Musical Family Collection** also written in two languages, English and Spanish.

Rocío Rodríguez es una arpista profesional y ha sido parte de numerosas orquestas sinfónicas en Canadá, Estados Unidos, Suecia, España, Colombia y Emiratos Árabes. Además, ella se ha interesado en la enseñanza musical de los más pequeños y por más de 20 años ha enseñado música con clases privadas y en diferentes instituciones educativas y musicales. A través de su enorme experiencia, Rocío ha diseñado un sistema de aprendizaje musical único, para que los niños en edad pre-escolar aprendan de manera rápida y divertida la lectura musical que servirá de base para empezar a tocar cualquier instrumento musical. Este sistema basado en diferentes métodos como Kodaly, Montessori, el sistema francés (solfeo) y el sistema inglés (notas con letras) se encuentra plasmado en la **Colección La Familia Musical** escrita además en dos idiomas, inglés y español.

The Musical Family Collection (Book 1: Rhythm, **Book 2: Notes**, Book 3: Measure, Book 4: Activity Book)
Colección La Familia Musical (Libro 1: Ritmo, **Libro 2: Notas**, Libro 3: Compás, Libro 4: Libro de Actividades)

Copyright © 2022 Rocío Rodríguez (Text and illustrations)
Cover Design: Imogen Phillips

All rights reserved
ISBN: 979-8-9870769-1-0
Printed in United States

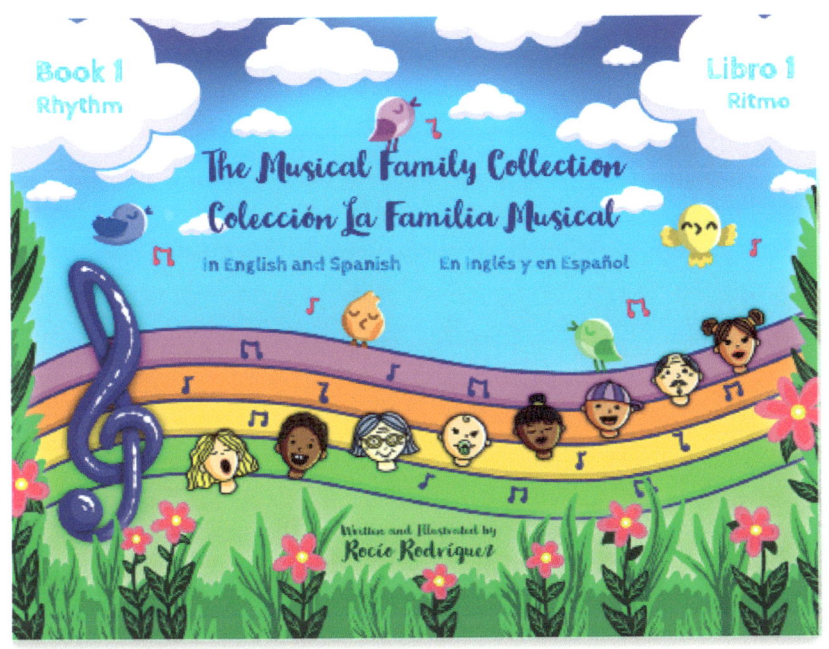

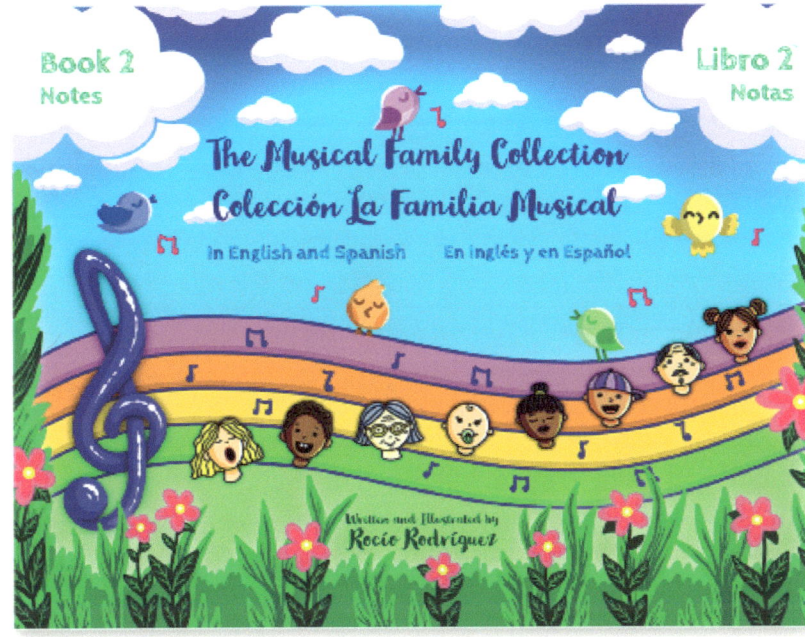

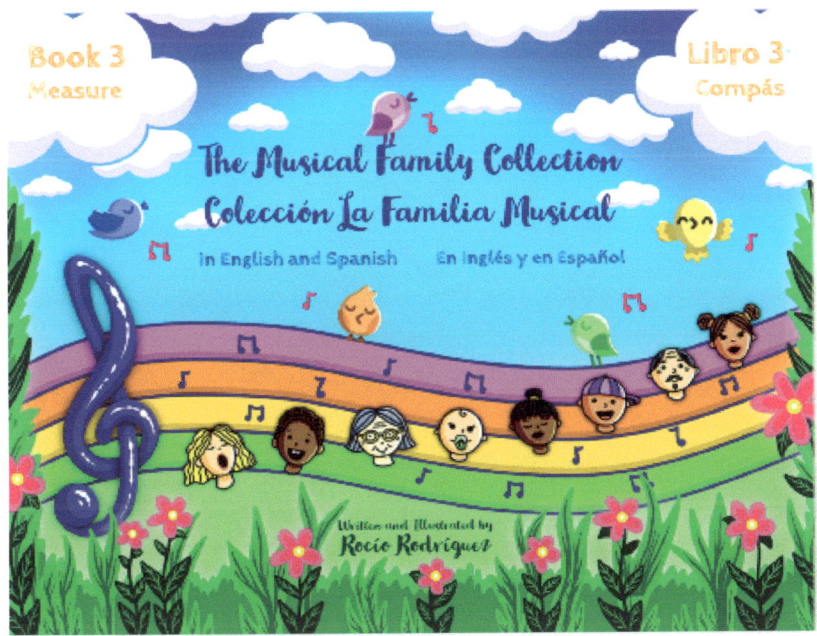

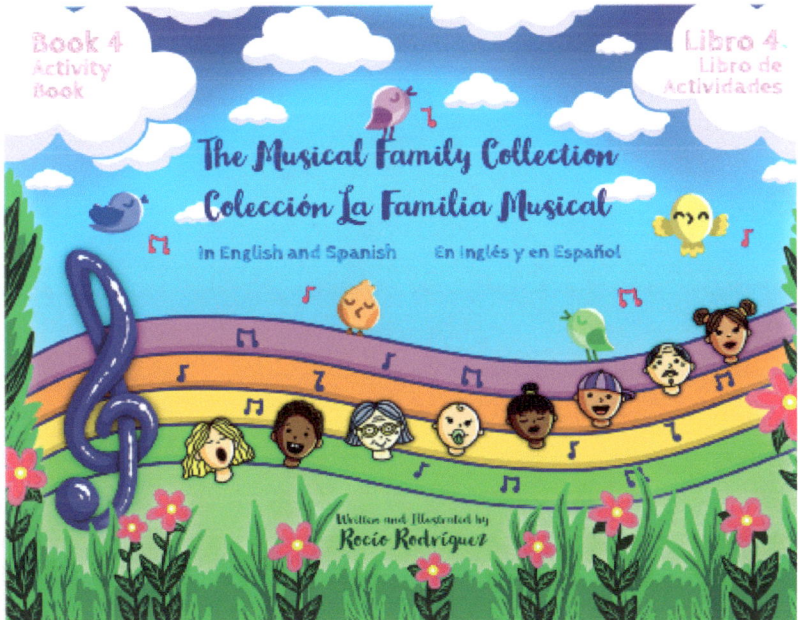

www.ingramcontent.com/pod-product-compliance
Lightning Source LLC
Chambersburg PA
CBHW040818120626

46551CB00004B/588

9 7 9 8 9 8 7 0 7 6 9 1 0